Second Edition
Saint Mary and Saint Mercurius church
Belleville NJ USA
908-760-6505
lazarus.of.alexandria@gmail.com
www.lazarusbook.org

Lazarus

LAZARUS

The Healing and Recovery of a Pornography Addict

"Consider what God has done: Who can straighten, what he has made crooked?" Ecclesiastes 7:13

Lazarus

Psalm 129:8,2
"Many a time they have afflicted me from my youth;
Yet they have not prevailed against me.
Neither let those who pass by them say,
"The blessing of the Lord be upon you;
We bless you in the name of the Lord!"

John 11:1-45
Now a certain man was sick, Lazarus of Bethany, the town of Mary and her sister Martha. It was that Mary who anointed the Lord with fragrant oil and wiped His feet with her hair, whose brother Lazarus was sick. Therefore the sisters sent to Him, saying, "Lord, behold, he whom You love is sick."
When Jesus heard that, He said, "This sickness is not unto death, but for the glory of God, that the Son of God may be glorified through it."
Now Jesus loved Martha and her sister and Lazarus. So, when He heard that he was sick, He stayed two more days in the place where He was. Then after this He said to the disciples, "Let us go to Judea again."
The disciples said to Him, "Rabbi, lately the Jews sought to stone You, and are You going there again?" Jesus answered, "Are there not twelve hours in the day? If anyone walks in the day, he does not stumble, because he sees the light of this world. But if one walks in the night, he stumbles, because the light is not in him." These things He said, and after that He said to them, "Our friend Lazarus sleeps, but I go that I may wake him up."
Then His disciples said, "Lord, if he sleeps he will get well." However, Jesus spoke of his death, but they thought that He was speaking about taking rest in sleep.
Then Jesus said to them plainly, "Lazarus is dead. And I am glad for your sakes that I was not

there, that you may believe. Nevertheless let us go to him."
Then Thomas, who is called the Twin, said to his fellow disciples, "Let us also go, that we may die with Him."
So when Jesus came, He found that he had already been in the tomb four days. Now Bethany was near Jerusalem, about two miles away. And many of the Jews had joined the women around Martha and Mary, to comfort them concerning their brother.
Now Martha, as soon as she heard that Jesus was coming, went and met Him, but Mary was sitting in the house. Now Martha said to Jesus, "Lord, if You had been here, my brother would not have died. But even now I know that whatever You ask of God, God will give You."
Jesus said to her, "Your brother will rise again."
Martha said to Him, "I know that he will rise again in the resurrection at the last day."
Jesus said to her, "I am the resurrection and the life. He who believes in Me, though he may die, he shall live. And whoever lives and believes in Me shall never die. Do you believe this?"
She said to Him, "Yes, Lord, I believe that You are the Christ, the Son of God, who is to come into the world."
And when she had said these things, she went her way and secretly called Mary her sister, saying, "The Teacher has come and is calling for you." As soon as she heard that, she arose quickly and came to Him. Now Jesus had not yet come into the town, but was[b] in the place where Martha met Him. Then the Jews who were with her in the house, and comforting her, when they saw that Mary rose up quickly and went out, followed her, saying, "She is going to the tomb to weep there."
Then, when Mary came where Jesus was, and saw Him, she fell down at His feet, saying to Him, "Lord,

if You had been here, my brother would not have died."
Therefore, when Jesus saw her weeping, and the Jews who came with her weeping, He groaned in the spirit and was troubled. And He said, "Where have you laid him?"
They said to Him, "Lord, come and see."
Jesus wept. Then the Jews said, "See how He loved him!"
And some of them said, "Could not this Man, who opened the eyes of the blind, also have kept this man from dying?"
Then Jesus, again groaning in Himself, came to the tomb. It was a cave, and a stone lay against it. Jesus said, "Take away the stone."
Martha, the sister of him who was dead, said to Him, "Lord, by this time there is a stench, for he has been dead four days."
Jesus said to her, "Did I not say to you that if you would believe you would see the glory of God?" Then they took away the stone from the place where the dead man was lying. And Jesus lifted up His eyes and said, "Father, I thank You that You have heard Me. And I know that You always hear Me, but because of the people who are standing by I said this, that they may believe that You sent Me." Now when He had said these things, He cried with a loud voice, "Lazarus, come forth!" And he who had died came out bound hand and foot with grave-clothes, and his face was wrapped with a cloth. Jesus said to them, "Loose him, and let him go."
Then many of the Jews who had come to Mary, and had seen the things Jesus did, believed in Him.
Amen

Lazarus

Jesus cried with a loud voice, "Lazarus, come forth!" John 11:43

**His Holiness Pope Tawadros II
118th Pope of Alexandria and
Patriarch of the See of St. Mark**

Lazarus

Table of Contents

Disclaimer 15
Preface 16
Coptic church* 18
Why I wrote this book 19
    Lazarus 20
    Self-justification 21
    Remembrance of evil 22
    God's work 22
    Alarm, hope & awareness 23
My Childhood 26
    Background 26
    Alone all the time 26
    Obesity 28
    Harassment 34
    Sinusitis 36
    Weak Vision 37
    School 38
    Mom 40
    Dad 42
    Grandparents 42
    Church 44
        Sunday School 44
        Serving as a Deacon 45
    Lack of Sexual Education 46
Teenage Years 50
    Innocent Curiosity 50
    Questions Without Answers 54
    The Internet 55

    Parental Control Software 58
    Alarming Signs and Neglect 60
    I am all Alone 61
    Bitter struggle 63
    Opposite Sex 64
    The Cycle of Death 65
    Middle School 66
Healing Journey 69
    Sunday School 69
    Camping and Adventure 70
    My Father of Confession 74
    Deaconship 76
    Spiritual Readings 76
    Service in Church 82
Lazarus, Come Forth! 87
    Recovery Period 91
        Prostrations (Metanyas) 91
        Tears 92
        Consistently Going to Confession 93
        Reading the Bible 94
        The Sign of the Cross 95
        Training My Sense of Sight 96
Advice in Raising Children 99
Conclusion 104

Lazarus

Disclaimer

This book is a memoir. It reflects the author's present recollections of experiences over time. Some names and identifying details have been changed to protect the privacy of individuals. Some events have been compressed, and some dialogues has been recreated.

Preface

Porn addiction is, without a doubt, one of Satan's main contemporary methods of destroying the image and likeness of God that is bestowed upon humans.

"Then God said, "Let Us make man in Our image, according to Our likeness; let them have dominion over the fish of the sea, over the birds of the air, and over the cattle, over all the earth and over every creeping thing that creeps on the earth." Genesis 1:26

St. Basil the Great explains the meaning of this gift to humans, making a distinction between God's image and His likeness. He says that we carry the image of God in three main attributes, namely, rational soul, free will, and authority ("let them have dominion ...."). As for the likeness of God, St. Basil explains that it pertains to humans' sharing with God His virtues, such as sacrificial love, joy, peace, etc.
People suffering from porn addiction quickly recognize that they gradually lose these attributes and virtues that make them look like God.

The staggering number of young men, young women, and adults who fall into this trap calls for a message of hope and liberty from this captivity. Thanks to our Lord, God and Savior Jesus Christ, who offered this to us through His incarnation and portrayed it in His mission statement when He said:

"The Spirit of the LORD is upon Me, Because He has anointed Me To preach the gospel to the poor; He has sent Me to heal the brokenhearted, To proclaim liberty to the captives And recovery of sight to the blind, To set at liberty those who are oppressed;" Luke 4:18

By the grace of God, as a Coptic Orthodox priest and a board certified addiction psychiatrist, I see the great value of Lazarus, which portrays this very strong message of hope. It is a well-written book, authored by an ex-porn addict who was able—with the love of God the Father, the grace of His Son, our Lord, God and Savior Jesus Christ, and the fellowship of the Holy Spirit—to conquer this monster which is porn addiction and get freed from it.

I personally know the author of Lazarus, and I admire his great work, effort, and zeal to share God's victory in him with his brothers and sisters in humanity who are under attack by porn addiction. I was blessed to revise Lazarus several times and found that it is a wonderful book that could be very helpful to any person who is suffering from this terrible condition. I pray to our Lord Jesus Christ that this book becomes a blessing to the salvation of many.

Fr. Luke Istafanous
M.D, A.B.P.N., A.B.A.M

Coptic church*

I was born and raised in Alexandria, Egypt; I have always known myself to be Coptic Christian. Let me introduce to you my beloved church, which was the main player in my salvation story.

Coptic Christians, known as Copts, are the largest religious minority in Egypt, constituting roughly 10 percent of the Egypt's 95 million people. Although many Egyptians are now identified as Arabs, Copts do not historically consider themselves to be of Arab origin; they instead acknowledge themselves as the remaining descendants of the civilization of the Ancient Egyptians, with Pharaonic origins. The word "Coptic" is derived from the ancient Greek word for Egyptian.

The Coptic Church is based on the teachings of Saint Mark, who brought Christianity to Egypt during the reign of the Roman emperor Nero in the first century, a dozen of years after the Lord's ascension. He was one of the four evangelists and the one who wrote the oldest canonical gospel.

Christianity spread throughout Egypt within half a century of Saint Mark's arrival in Alexandria, as is clear from the New Testament writings found in Bahnasa, in Middle Egypt, which date around the year 200 A.D., and a fragment of the Gospel of Saint John, written using the Coptic language, which was found in Upper Egypt and can be dated to the first half of the second century. The Coptic Church, which is now more than nineteen centuries old, was the subject of many prophecies in the Old Testament. Isaiah the prophet, in Chapter 19, Verse 19 says, *"In that day there will be an altar to the LORD in the midst of the land of Egypt, and a pillar to the LORD at its border."*

*http://www.coptic.net/EncyclopediaCoptica

Why I wrote this book.

This book is a testimony of God's work in my life. My Lord Jesus Christ redeemed my life from destruction and saved me from death in sin.

This book is a narrative of my experience during my childhood and teenage years, so that people can read it and avoid the same mistakes that I made.

This book is a wake-up call for all parents to realize how vicious Satan's war on their children is so they can stand in support, defending and strengthening their children. The biggest betrayal parents commit is ignoring their children's suffering and leaving them fighting for their holiness and purity on their own. *"Therefore, to him who knows to do good and does not do it, to him it is sin." James 4:17.*

This book is a message of hope to everyone struggling in his/her purity and chastity battle. Do not ever lose hope and don't believe Satan's lies. I was in the same exact situation, if not worse. I was practicing defiling habits, longing to fill my *"stomach with the pods that the pigs were eating" Luke 15:16.* I was addicted to pornography; but even more, I was doing evil by practicing masturbation. But my Lord redeemed my life from destruction and raised me from death in sin by a heavenly miracle that I will describe in detail. Believe me, that no matter how bad your situation is or how enslaved to sin you are, God is able to save you by His miraculous work. Because *"where sin abounded, grace abounded much more, so that as sin reigned in death, even so grace might reign through righteousness to eternal life through Jesus Christ our Lord." Romans 5:20.* Our Lord Jesus Christ is alive and works daily to save us from slavery and death in sin. *"For God so loved the world that He gave His only begotten Son, that whoever believes in Him should not perish but have everlasting life." John 3:16.*

Finally, this book is a message for all servants and youth ministers in church to realize the importance of sexual education. This topic should be addressed in Sunday school regularly; once a year is not enough. Servants, please realize you might be the only source of reliable, accurate information in a world full of lies. Please do not shy away from talking about sexual education. Our children are perishing from negligence and lack of correct information. *"My people are destroyed for lack of knowledge" Hosea 4:6.*

Lazarus

I would like to introduce myself: My name is Lazarus. I chose this name because my story is identical to the story of Lazarus in the Bible. I died morally and all hope in my return to life was lost to the point of burial in a tomb, until Jesus *"cried with a loud voice, "Lazarus, come forth!"" John 11:43.* This book is a summary of twelve years I spent buried in the tomb of addiction to pornography and masturbation. The best years of my life and the finest days in my youth were lost to sex addiction. God allowed this to happen but this *"sickness is not unto death, but for the glory of God, that the Son of God may be glorified through it." John 11:4.*

Amen! I believe that God allowed me to go through this tribulation to be a source of help to people suffering from pornography addiction. God saved me from bitter bondage and I will remain indebted to God all of my life, and nothing can pay back this debt. Many days, months and years went by while I was still trapped inside the tomb of sexual addiction. I repeatedly cried bitterly saying, "Where are you God? Why are you leaving me alone? I don't want this defilement." I was like Mary and Martha, crying in tears saying, *"Lord, if you had been here, my brother would not have died." John 11:32.* Constantly, I sat by the tomb, weeping from my bondage, feeling great desperation, unable to find my way out of this slavery. Back then, I felt as if I was crying all by myself and nobody cared about me. Now I realized that *"Jesus wept." John 11:35*. Jesus wept just like I was weeping, but I couldn't see Him because I was too self-centered. God used my fiancée to take away the stone from the door of the tomb and by a word from his mouth, *"he who had died came out bound hand and foot with grave clothes, and his face was wrapped with a cloth." John 11:44*.

Finally, I went through a recovery phase where God's servants freed me from any remaining bondages.

I don't blame anyone
Before delving into my story, let me clarify a few things:

Self-justification
First of all, I am not trying to portray myself as a victim of society or circumstances. Rather the opposite, I take full responsibility for every second that I lived in sin. While it is true that my circumstances were less than perfect, I could have still avoided a lot of mistakes and I could have been quicker in repenting and striving diligently. I am not seeking in any way to justify myself or to blame or point the finger at other people. Jesus taught us, *"Hypocrite! First remove the plank from your own eye, and then you will see clearly to remove the speck from your brother's eye." Matthew 7:5*.

Throughout the book, I will address some parenting mistakes or maltreatment that I was exposed to from my parents, as well as abuse I suffered from other people. I have forgiven them completely and I love them sincerely. I am not addressing these mistakes to blame anyone, but to give a complete picture of my circumstances so people can learn from these mistakes and not repeat them. Again, I confess before everyone that I am the only one responsible for my sins. *"He who covers his sins will not prosper, but whoever confesses and forsakes them will have mercy." Proverbs 28:13.*

Remembrance of evil

Secondly, I do not intend through this book to describe details of sin or explain sinful ideas for people suffering from temptation, but rather the opposite. *"Jesus said to his disciples: 'Things that cause people to stumble are bound to come, but woe to anyone through whom they come.'" Luke 1:17.* I don't want to fill my *"stomach with the pods that the pigs were eating" Luke 15:16* again, and as we pray in Saint Basil's liturgy, "save us from the remembrance of evil entailing death." I will not describe any sinful details and I will be very brief if the context requires details.

God's work

Finally, I don't intend to present myself as a hero who overcame addiction by my willpower. On the contrary, all the credit goes to Christ. My Lord Jesus saved me from the Devil's slavery by the grace of the Holy Spirit. If anything could be counted as effort on my part, it would be my deep hatred to the sin I was committing and my continuous crying out to Jesus so he would save me from this slavery. I repeatedly cried with Saint Paul saying, *"O wretched man that I am! Who will deliver me from this body of death?" Romans 7:24.* In the right time, Christ intervened and raised me from death in sin.

Alarm, hope & awareness

I have explained what I don't want from this book. What I am looking to achieve through this book is the following:

First, to offer hope for everyone trapped in this bitter slavery. Believe that God can heal you through his miraculous work. Don't postpone repentance; stand up ***now*** and repent like the prodigal son and tell Jesus *"I will arise and go to my father, and will say to him, "Father, I have sinned against heaven and before you" Luke 15:18*. Repentance can occur anytime and anywhere. *"Behold, now* is *the accepted time; behold, now* is *the day of salvation." 2 Corinthians 6:2*. Leave this book and lift up your heart to your Savior ***now***. Go see your father of confession ***now***.

Secondly, to raise awareness among parents and Sunday school servants; our children are facing a vicious war from evil powers seeking to make them disabled and injured. Let me mention some facts*:

- 93% of males and 62% of females are exposed to pornographic material before the age of 18
- The average age for first exposure to pornographic material is 11
- Only 3% of males and 17% of females never saw pornographic material
- The majority of pornography consumers range in age from 12 to 17
- 70% of males and 23% of females saw a pornographic movie longer than 30 minutes
- 48% of teenagers are exposed to pornography without looking for it on purpose
- The money spent on the pornographic industry is estimated to be 10 billion USD

*The Nature and Dynamics of Internet Pornography Exposure for Youth by Chiara Sabina, Ph.D.,1 Janis Wolak, J.D.,2 and David Finkelhor, Ph.D.2

It is our duty these days to worry about our children, as they are facing this fierce battle; they can't face it by themselves. Our children are victims of evil powers. In short, this book is a strong cry. I don't want to see the new generations disturbed and enslaved like I was. I urge you to *"Be sober, be vigilant; because your adversary the devil walks about like a roaring lion, seeking whom he may devour"* (1Peter 5:8).

Lazarus

My Childhood
Background

I was born into a financially stable family. We started as working class then climbed up the social ladder to the upper class. We used to live in a rich neighborhood. My parents worked in well-paid jobs and they frequently traveled for business. My parents spent most of their day at work and when they returned home, they talked on the phone about work or talked together about work. My parents were very busy with their successful careers and always hired a nanny to do housekeeping.

Alone all the time
Being an only child and the pain of loneliness

I was an only child and always lonely. God did not arrange for me to have brothers or sisters. I never knew the reason why I was always lonely. Whether it was my parents' will or for health reasons, I don't know. I don't care about the reason nor do I want to search for the reason, lest I fall into judging my parents. My loneliness as a child and my parents' constant occupation with their careers was the perfect mix for assuring an inferiority complex inside me.

I frequently cried many tears saying, "I want a brother! I am not happy living alone!" Mom would look annoyed, turn her face the other side, and get out of the room without answering me. I repeated the same question many times and I waited in vain for a convincing answer. Many times, I would really pressure my parents to get me a brother, but nothing happens. I even asked for a pet and they refused. I was always ignored and left alone crying, and usually a mediator (one of my relatives or my grandparents) would show up and calm down my anger without any involvement from my parents.

In the afternoons, I always wanted to play with my parents, but many times they had business appointments or dinner late at night. Mom and Dad would come home exhausted after work. They would eat dinner then go to the bedroom for a nap. I would patiently wait for them to finish their nap so I can play with them. Frequently, I would be so disappointed because they are taking me to Grandma's house, as that meant them going to work or a business dinner at night time. When I realized that they are taking me to Grandma's house and leaving, I would break down in tears saying, "I want Mom and Dad." They would not answer and I would run fast to the door and Grandma would calm me down. It was heartbreaking and I still vividly recall the scenes in my mind until this day.

I lived most of my childhood with my grandparents. I was their first grandchild and you can imagine the amount of pampering that I received. I don't blame my grandparents for this. If I had the choice, I would have chosen to stay more with my parents without any pampering instead of staying most of the time with my grandparents. I had a deep longing to stay with my parents; I had great admiration for them, but I couldn't spend time with them because they were always busy with work. I had deep pain inside me because of their constant absence—a strong feeling settled inside me that I am not welcomed or loved. I received a strong message saying: "Career is more important than you; man up and stop whining." Negligence and disregard created a profound hurt inside me; I still suffer from it until now. Day after day, this sense of inferiority kept on increasing until it became a part of me, and I felt inferior every day and every moment.

To all parents, your child doesn't need your money; he/she needs YOU, your time, your attention, and your love. Trust me, the best gift to your child is time. The Bible says *"Fathers, do not provoke your children, lest they become discouraged." Colossians 3:2.* Negligence and disregard creates an agonizing feeling of anger. Please take care of your children. Until now—even after I grew up and became a father—whenever I look at my children playing together, I get emotional. I feel that I am missing what my children are enjoying from friendship and brotherhood. Whenever I look at a group of brothers and sisters playing together, I wish that I could join them. A message for all people angry with their siblings: you own a great treasure. I wish I had half of what you have. Reconcile with your siblings. You have a big blessing that I was deprived of.

Obesity

I lived the first five years of my life with my grandparents most of the time. During these five years, I never dealt with any child my age, so I was shocked when I went to school. I expected other children at school to treat me the same way as Grandma! Excessive spoiling by my grandparents made me arrogant. I failed in dealing with my classmates and I ended up isolated. Yes, isolated! I never had any friends and I used to walk slowly all by myself during recess eating my sandwiches. Being obese made things worse and increased my isolation. I am a classic example of my generation; I used to spend long hours watching TV with Grandma, followed by food, then back to watching TV till bedtime. Rarely did I do any physical activity, and the result was severe obesity that increased my isolation.

Consequently, isolation led to inferiority complex and confirmed my daily feeling of shame because I was not liked by my classmates. Nobody ever wanted to play with me because I was arrogant, complicated, and did not know how to play soccer. Many of my classmates used to call me names because I was fat. I used to fight with them, but I lost because

I was weak. I lived in shame of obesity all of my life. I never knew myself slim. I endured a lot of bullying at school and nobody defended me!

I remember one day, I started lying to my parents about imaginary athletic achievements as a defense mechanism to numb the psychological pain from obesity. I was narrating these lies to my parents because I was desperate for appreciation. I knew that I was lying to my parents, but the psychological pain was unbearable; thus, I desperately sought to be appreciated to kill the pain, regardless of the means. I completely failed in getting my classmates to like me and I lived every day in isolation, suffering from shame until I adapted and got used to my situation.

A call to all servants and teachers: never neglect any socially withdrawn child. Social withdrawal is a clear sign of psychological suffering. Give attention to socially withdrawn children without giving any advice; introverted children know their problems very well and don't need to be repeatedly reminded of them. Real care for social isolation comes by creating a relationship with the child and through words of encouragement. If you talk with these types of children, you will find many hidden talents. Show them their talents; they might not realize their value due to repeated criticism and lack of self-confidence. Please don't deprive yourself of being a healing tool in the hands of the True Physician. Finally, don't overlook socially withdrawn children, as Solomon said, *"Be diligent to know the state of your flocks, and attend to your herds" (Proverbs 27-23).*

Shame of obesity was chasing me everywhere I go, even at home.
Mom with a loud voice: "Lazarus enough eating!"
Me (having a sad, oppressed face): "Mom, I'm hungry"
Mom: "You ate a lot, Lazarus"
Grandma would come interrupting the exchange, yelling at Mom: "What's going on! Let him eat!"
They both stare at each other with anger and the conversation ends.

At this moment I thought that I love Mom and I want to be obedient to her, but what happened? Yesterday, I could have eaten whatever I want! Why did Grandma disagree with Mom? I don't understand! Why are they fighting because of me? I love them both and don't want them to fight.

This event would happen over and over again, especially when I used to spend the summer with my grandparents. The first thing Mom would tell me after getting home was, "You gained weight!"

I was expecting Mom to welcome me with a hug and tell me, "I miss you! What did you do at Grandma's house?" On the contrary, the first thing she told me was a negative comment about my body.

I experienced the ultimate shame when I heard all my family members talking about my obesity. Conversations were always heated and a feeling of confusion was dominating the scene, as if they were saying, "We are puzzled because of you, Lazarus. We don't know what to do!" I used to hate myself in these situations and I wished I could disappear from their sight. I used to stand up silent, and a feeling of guilt controlled me. I want my family to love me, but I can't change my body.

As I grew older, my body became more and more obese and ugly. I hated looking in the mirror and hated buying new clothes. People's looks in clothing stores were killing me and Mom used to tell me, "See we can't buy you nice clothing because you are fat! See this nice shirt, we can't buy it because we can't find your size." I regularly heard store employees saying, "Oh! For him we need adult sizes! No child size would fit!"

Random people that I didn't know would come to me saying negative comments like, "Oh! You elephant!" "Such a big fat dolphin;" "Hey, you pig!" I used to get really annoyed, and I rarely answered back. I recall being in a train with a group of teenagers sitting in the next wagon, and on my way to the bathroom, these teenagers saw me. I can see them gazing at me and talking, and on my way back to my seat, one of the boys came to me saying, "You eat well at home!" All the girls laughed! I gave him a stern look and left, but I didn't know why everyone was against me! Am I that bad?!

In an attempt to lose weight, my parents decided that I should practice sports. First, my parents decided that I would play tennis and I started going regularly to tennis practice. Then, my parents decided that I should do swimming and I started going regularly to tennis and swimming practice. Then, my parents decided that I should play basketball, and I started going regularly to tennis, swimming and basketball practice! I never chose any of these sports; they were all forced on me. I felt that going to practice was punishment for a mistake that I didn't do! They forced me to go to practice because I was fat, which I felt was unjustified because being fat was supposedly a bad thing, and I wasn't bad! Then I would break in tears. I didn't understand why I was fat. I used to think that God created me this way, so why didn't they like me?

Repeatedly, I felt great anxiety before practice time, to the point where my stomach would start hurting. I felt that I was going for a punishment that I didn't deserve. Once, this discussion happened:

> Me, in tears, saying: "Mom, my stomach hurts badly," and it was really hurting.
> Mom: "Stop acting! We are going to practice anyway!"
> Me: "I am not lying; my stomach really hurts"
> Mom: "WE ARE GOING TO PRACTICE!"

The pain would continue for a couple of minutes, then disappear, and when we returned home after practice, my mom would tell Dad, "Lazarus is pretending to be sick so we don't go to practice."

Overall, I failed in losing weight by practicing sports because I wasn't complementing sports with a nutritional diet. However, to be fair and reasonable, practicing sports had a positive impact on my life. At least, I learned swimming and over time, I learned many skills in tennis that increased my self-confidence. However, basketball was a complete failure. Practicing sports didn't have any tangible short-term effect, but its long term effect was worthwhile. These trainings increased my overall fitness and helped me a lot later in life.

Actually, the short-term effect of practicing sports was destructive because the result was that I practiced sports and still remained obese! Thus, shame of failure was added to the shame of obesity. I vividly recall one of my relatives approaching me saying, "How are you doing in tennis.... and swimming.... and Basketball...." Then, he had a long, sarcastic laugh!

The idea of practicing sports was theoretically correct; however, the way it was done made it a disappointment. Dear parents, make your child's sport practice successful by doing the following:

- Practicing sports should be done for the right reasons. Losing weight in my opinion is not the right reason because it won't work unless complemented with a nutritional diet. The right reasons for practicing sports should be building your children's character and skills, and giving them a good way to spend their free time.

- Let your children freely choose the sport they like and don't force them into a specific sport. If your child can't decide, be supportive and observe his/her skills; there is no harm in trying different sports without any pressure. Don't deal with your child as a guinea pig trying different things without understanding his/her personality. We don't respect our children and this is a huge mistake. Your children are God's children. You are held accountable for them in front of God. Respect them and don't ignore or offend them. *"Then He said to the disciples, "It is impossible that no offenses should come, but woe to him through whom they do come! It would be better for him if a millstone were hung around his neck, and he were thrown into the sea, than that he should offend one of these little ones." (Luke 17:1-2)*
- Practicing only one sport is enough.
- Watch them during practice and be supportive and encouraging. Also, protect your child. Some coaches are abusive and mean.
- Positive words have a magical effect. Be supportive and encouraging to boost your child's self-confidence. *"Comfort the fainthearted, uphold the weak, be patient with all" (1 Thessalonians 5:14)*

Finally, dear parent, let me ask you: which is more important, your child's morale, self-esteem and self-confidence, or sports or grades at school or …. or ….. or ….. ?

As parents, we tend to set the wrong priorities for our children and they suffer the consequences.

Harassment

I forgot to talk about Judo. I was in my last year in elementary school and this time, it was my choice to practice Judo, hoping for weight loss and self-confidence. I was dreaming to succeed in this sport because it didn't require a skinny body. Judo practice consisted of a long period of cardio exercises, followed by teaching martial arts. I used to spend a lot of effort in these classes and at the end of each class, I used to be completely exhausted, very sweaty, and stinky. My father advised me to shower after class. I didn't like to do so because only adult Judo players did that. However, I listened to Dad and I showered after every class. I used the adult showering facility because I wanted to mimic adults, and I didn't feel secure with the young players because of bullying.

Everything went fine until one day, I used the young players showering facility. While showering, one of my peers opened the shower curtain and started looking at my naked body. Then he left me and started shouting, "Somebody is showering," as if he found a hidden treasure or precious opportunity. I didn't say a word and I was extremely shy and embarrassed. He came a second time, looked at my naked, ugly and chubby body, and left shouting the same words as if he was looking for a partner in his crime. I was ashamed and embarrassed; I didn't know what to do and I wished the whole situation would end. Then, he came a third time and stayed longer, singing, "Oh shower! Oh shower!" while looking at my naked body. His face was full of evil looks, biting his lips and winking. I didn't understand any of his sexual gestures. Finally, I screamed in his face, "You're impolite!" He repeated my words with sarcasm and left laughing victoriously. I didn't finish my shower; I got dressed and left the facility crying. I truly thank God that he didn't find a partner in crime and that he didn't sexually abuse me. God saved me in this bad situation. Had it not been for God's care, I could have suffered more.

I warn all servants in the Coptic church, especially those in charge of retreat buildings, that this situation could easily be repeated in retreat houses. I recommend the following:

- All showers should have locked doors, and not just curtains.
- There should be adult supervision during shower time.
- Raise awareness about sexual harassment so children can defend themselves. I was weak and reacted slowly after the third time.

I never told my father what happened. I just told him a general idea that people see me while I am showering and I never used the young players showering facility again.

I continued going to Judo classes, learning some skills, and becoming more self-confident. One day, I decided to walk in the street wearing my Judo uniform. I was proud of my uniform, but it ended up being a parade of public humiliation. During 10 minutes of walking in the street, I was bullied and harassed more than 10 times! I remember hearing, "Hey, you chubby!" and "Kiddo! Come here, I will beat you up!" I wondered why people would not leave me alone. Do I look that ugly? I didn't talk to anyone; I was just walking in the street. I was suffering shame because of obesity; I was struggling to gain self-confidence and now all of my inner doubts are confirmed.

I am ugly because I am fat. Nobody loves me because I am fat. Even people that I don't know talk negatively about me! I believed that I was ugly and unloved, and I dealt with obesity as a fact of life that I couldn't change. No matter what

I do, I will remain fat, ugly and unloved. I never tried practicing any sports again and I lived all of my life suffering from obesity. This is an example of when society becomes very negative and destructive: killing the dream before it is born and aborting any chance of personal advancement.

Sinusitis

As mentioned before, my self-image was very negative because I believed I was an untalented ugly person. What made things even worse was sinusitis; 90% of the time, I was suffering from a stuffy nose and breathing from my mouth. I have seen many doctors, but nothing helped. I suffered from severe sinus allergy and the only thing that offered some relief was nasal spray.

Sinusitis caused me a lot of embarrassment with my classmates. Eventually, I got used to my peers' bullying, and I never bothered anymore or expected anything nice from my classmates.

The sound of blowing my nose (which is something I used to do very frequently) was loud, to the point where I got used to seeing the whole class laughing loudly every time I blew my nose. One day, I was blowing my nose and a teacher yelled, "Enough!" and the whole class broke in laughter.

I remember one of my classmates drawing a caricature of me as fat person holding a tissue, with mucus dropping out of my nose. He wrote under it, "Mucus factory!"

I never heard any comforting words from my school peers; laughter and bullying dominated the scene. I always felt I had nothing to do with this. Why do people laugh at your illness? None of the teachers cared to understand the problem or even defend me against the bullying. I was bullied under the eyes of teachers and nobody helped me—only yelling and disregard.

It was known among my peers that I borrow lots of tissues. The reason was that sinusitis made me blow my nose at least 10 times a day! It took me a while to understand my condition and be prepared with a big pack of tissues every day. Meanwhile, I was known as the tissue-borrower! My classmates used to call me, "Lazarus, can I borrow a tissue!"

I became a very sensitive person, afraid of dealing with people, very shy, and keeping conversations to minimum lest, I get bullied. Constantly, I would break in tears for trivial reasons and frequently, I misunderstood a simple situation because I was expecting to be bullied.

Weak Vision

I wasn't able to copy the teacher's notes from the blackboard. I had to move to the front to be able to see the writing and copy the teacher's notes. The Arabic teacher was the first to notice my weak vision and she told me to go see an eye doctor. I didn't listen to her because I didn't like her. This teacher was so unpleasant; she never smiles, always carried the beating stick, and used to hit us with the sharp side of the stick. After her beatings, my hands used to feel numb, tingling like pins and needles going through my hand. This teacher used to beat us for every mistake! Do anything wrong, you will get beaten! Forget the copybook—2 hits on each hand. Didn't do the homework—4 hits on each hand, and so on! This teacher used to repeatedly tell me, "Go see an eye doctor," till one day, she had enough and yelled, "I SAID TELL YOUR PARENTS TO SEE AN EYE DOCTOR." I still didn't listen because I didn't like her, and I felt she didn't care about me; I figured she was only bothered by me moving to the front to copy the notes.

One day, Dad realized that I couldn't read the road signs and he was shocked. He took me to the doctor and I cried a lot when I realized I needed to wear glasses; I completely rejected any additional weaknesses to my situation. My inner voice would say, "I have enough negatives and weaknesses and I also need to wear glasses?!?"

Severe sensitivity and breaking in tears became part of who I am. My parents used to tell me, "Stop being a girl. Why do you cry a lot?" They always wanted me to shut up, without understanding my suffering. My parents didn't want to have problems. By time, I adapted to emotional pain and I believed that I was ugly. I lived with low self-esteem and no self-confidence.

I thank my Lord for these tribulations. God was preparing a precise treatment plan and I believe all of this happened for the glory of His name. I don't have any grudge or hatred towards anyone, and everything that happened was through God's permission. I am not writing these sections to retaliate, but to lay down facts, so people can learn from these mistakes; I hate seeing children suffer from overly sensitive personalities and low self-confidence. I believe that *"all things work together for good to those who love God, to those who are the called according to His purpose" (Romans 8:28).* I also believe that people didn't realize how harmful bullying is; I hope we avoid these mistakes in future generations.

School

My parents gave high priority to my education, and consequently, they had sent me to an expensive private school. Tuition was a big challenge for my parents, but they managed to deal with it. I am deeply grateful to them for caring about my education; this helped me a lot later in life.

School was disciplined and organized, very strict especially in anything concerning behavior. There was a lot of physical abuse, and relationships with teachers were based on fear. Every teacher invented his own way of beating the students! The typical way was stick beating; others used to pull our hair and forcefully shake our heads; some teachers used to pull our ears. Each teacher used to have his own beating stick; the bigger, the better, and punishment was mainly through physical abuse.

Overall, educational standards were very high, especially in the languages. However, the atmosphere was filled with fear—something not healthy for a wounded personality like mine. I wasn't a trouble maker at school. I was shy, quiet, and very scared of the teacher's beating stick.

I recall that they once changed the class schedule and I was surprised that the first period was science and I didn't have the science book. I started crying, scared of getting beaten, and my classmates started to calm me. The teacher understood, but she was stunned because I cried a lot, so she yelled at me saying, "Enough crying! I am not going to beat you!" Another day, I got beaten 10 times on my hand for forgetting my calligraphy notebook.

To be fair, a small number of teachers didn't beat us and used extra homework as a punishment instead, which was a brilliant idea! We learned and memorized the lessons and never tried to repeat same mistake. Thus, this type of punishment would have a double effect, with neither humiliation for student nor hard feelings from student towards teacher. Honestly, I am thankful for teachers who didn't use corporal punishment; there is always light in the midst of darkness.

I got a good education, but the overall atmosphere was frightening. I am completely against corporal punishment; I believe it's weak and ineffective. There are many smarter ways to punish, ways that are more effective and maintain the child's dignity. Examples include timeout, detention, denial of a specific privilege, and an increased workload. Beating seems to be effective, but has very harmful long-term effects. Let us respect our children and stop beating them.

Mom

My relationship with Mom was lacking in tenderness; I recall throwing myself in her arms and starting to kiss her arms, hoping that she would hug me and give me a kiss, but nothing happened.

The general foundation for my relationship with Mom was studying. She would strictly enforce study time, and many times, she would yell at me because I didn't want to study. Mom used to spend a lot of time with me studying, explaining concepts, and doing extra homework. She bought me extra books. made me do extra exercises, and explained additional information beyond the school curriculum. I am grateful to her from the bottom of my heart, as she taught me to be a hard worker.

However, her emphasis on school and studying motivated me to excel in this direction solely to please her and made studies and school my main source of self-confidence. This is because I lost any hope in any other source of self-confidence. I was fat, ugly, suffered daily from embarrassing sinusitis, socially isolated, and lacked friends. All doors for self-satisfaction were blocked and I had only God to rely on as the real source for happiness and self-esteem. I eagerly searched for good grades, as this was the only remaining source for satisfaction and appreciation. Truly, this verse applied to me: *"For My people have committed two evils: They have forsaken Me, the fountain of living waters,* And *hewn themselves cisterns—broken cisterns that can hold no water"(Jeremiah 2:13)*.

Finally, the report card came. I was one of the top 5 students in my class and I was so happy. Then, I looked at Mom, waiting for a word of encouragement or a big hug to boost my morale and self-esteem. She looked at me and said, "I succeeded! Not you!" Implicitly, my mother was saying that all merit goes to her for my grades, that I was nothing! If it wasn't for her forcing me to study, I would have failed. I lost the value of success and I seriously considered intentionally failing the exams, but I was afraid of the consequences. I lost any motivation for success. I was getting good grades because of Mom, but I was never self-motivated; if Mom didn't force me, I wouldn't do it myself.

Dear parents, please never exaggerate your care for school grades; if Mom had spent the same effort she did in a spiritual direction, I wouldn't have ended up being a pornography addict. *"For what will it profit a man if he gains the whole world, and loses his own soul?" (Mark 8:36).* Please, honestly answer these questions; do I give the same priority to spirituality as school grades? Is going to church the same priority as going to school? Do I spend as much time with my son reading the Bible as I spend time studying? Good grades will never satisfy your children; I have seen university professors who are mentally ill and businessmen suffering from inferiority complexes that kill them. When we die, Jesus won't say, "Come, you blessed of My Father, inherit the kingdom prepared for you from the foundation of the world because you had good grades" or "Come, you blessed of My Father, inherit the kingdom prepared for you from the foundation of the world because you were rich." If money is a priority in life, why did Jesus say, *"Assuredly, I say to you that it is hard for a rich man to enter the kingdom of heaven. And again I say to you, it is easier for a camel to go through the eye of a needle than for a rich man to enter the kingdom of God." (Matthew 19:23-24)*

Dad

My relationship with Dad was full of mutual respect. I remember asking him lots of questions, and he always answered patiently and honestly. He contributed a great deal to building my character and he repeatedly told me, "You are a good boy." His words used to give me relief and hope. Again, words of encouragement have a magical effect. The Bible says, *"Pleasant speech multiplies friends, and gracious lips, friendly greetings." (Wisdom of Sirach 6:5).*

A friendship grew between Dad and me because of his patience in answering all of my questions and his positive encouraging words, but things changed because Dad became busier with his career. He used to come home exhausted, and he didn't have any time to spend with me. Furthermore, exhaustion made his patience disappear. His positive words and encouragement were replaced with yelling, and in some cases, beatings for very trivial reasons. This huge inconsistency, resulting from work stress, left me perplexed and confused. I didn't understand why Dad's dealings changed dramatically, until I realized the link between Dad's temperament and work stress.

Grandparents

My grandparents played the major role in my upbringing. I used to spend most of the time with them during summer, and during winter, I stayed with Grandma after school till Mom and Dad returned from work. Then, it was homework time. I saw in my grandma a true example of a righteous spiritual woman. She never told me to pray, but I watched her praying daily with Grandpa. Raising our children by example is easier and more effective than talking and punishing. Indeed, Pope Shenouda said once, "Our children don't grow up as we like them to be, but as we actually are." Saint Paul said, *"Be an example to the believers in word, in conduct, in love, in spirit, in faith, in purity" (1 Timothy 4:12).*

I saw my grandparents on a daily basis meeting to read the Bible, then listening to a Bible commentary on the radio, then ending their meeting by praying from the Agpeya.* Every morning, I saw my grandma sitting in the balcony and praying from the Agpeya, and when done, she would work on her household duties. My grandma was the first to explain to me how to use the Agpeya and the first to introduce me to the Bible. I will never forget that day; I got so excited that I can read the Bible, just like Grandma. Grandma used to tell me stories of saints and she introduced me to the Synaxarium.**

Grandma and Grandpa used to happily tolerate me when I acted out. I remember one day, I wanted Grandpa to play with me and he was holding the Agpeya praying. I started trying to catch the Agpeya so that he would stop praying. Grandpa tried to stop me, but I was quicker than him, and finally, I grasped the Agpeya book. I found him still reciting the prayers, as he memorized all the Agpeya prayers. I saw my grandparents praying wholeheartedly during trials and tribulations. Grandpa encouraged me to be a deacon; he took me to liturgy and explained to me what to do. I saw my grandparents praying for each family member individually by name. They endured the pain of illness in extraordinary thankfulness and gratitude. Grandpa, especially, had extraordinary humility, and I remember he was the first to teach me generosity and sharing.

---

*Agpeya is a Coptic word that means "Prayer book of hours." It's primarily composed of Psalm readings from the Old Testament and gospel readings from the New Testament, with some added hymns of praise,
**Synaxarium is the name given to the book that compiles the lives of Saints and Martyrs, along with some Church-related events, arranged in the order of their anniversaries.

I used to refuse sharing my plate with anyone, and when he saw that, he started eating from my plate and I got angry and said "no." Then, my mother came and told me (most likely as part of a plan with Grandpa): "No big deal Lazarus, you can share with Grandpa; you should be generous!" It was a practical lesson in sharing and generosity. I used to go regularly to church with my grandparents. Definitely, they were the ones who planted the seed of faith in my life. I was saved from pornography addiction because of their prayers. Thank you, Lord—I am so lucky because of my grandparents.

Church
Sunday School

I started attending Sunday school regularly at an old age, because when I was younger, my parents gave priority to family visits over bringing me to Sunday school.

In spite of that, I had a strong spiritual foundation because my grandparents read me the Bible and told me stories of the saints on a daily basis. In church, I found a healthy environment. They accepted me as I am, without any prejudgment or negative comments. No one mocked my weight, and no one mocked my sinusitis. I was welcomed and loved. I have never forgotten the outreach visits to my house; they were few, but very effective and memorable. I faced some bullying in church, but it was minimal; the servants always interfered and defended me, contrary to the neglect from the school teachers. I heard a lot of praise in church that relieved my pain and reduced my anger. Church was truly a harbor of salvation that played a major role in healing my pain. If I was introduced to church at an earlier age, my situation would have definitely been much better. Unfortunately, I got to know the church at a late stage, when low self-esteem and lack of self-respect controlled me completely. Church was a daily painkiller, but true healing required longer time. I am thankful to God, wholeheartedly, for His house.

Serving as a Deacon

The first person who called me to serve as a deacon was one of my church fathers. Then, my Grandpa bought me a Tunic (Tonya,*) and I remember Abouna** telling me to memorize three sentences: "look towards the east", "those who are seated stand," and "stand up for prayer." I went to the liturgy to serve as a deacon the first time; I was so shy and afraid, but Abouna asked one of the older deacons to take care of me and made me respond in the microphone, "Those who are seated stand." I said it very quickly and with no rhythm. In spite of this, Abouna told me after liturgy, in front of Grandpa, "Lazarus is a very good boy, but next time talk slowly and with rhythm." I was so shy and afraid, but I really felt welcomed, and thanks to my parents' encouragement, I loved serving as a deacon and became a disciple to the righteous elder deacons. I learned everything concerning the altar rites from them.

With time, I memorized all the altar deacon responses and I knew the censer rites. I also memorized the Gospel of the Third Hour and regularly prayed it before the Procession of the Lamb, and as I grew, I started reading one of the five readings during the Liturgy of the Word. I loved going to liturgy and preferred going very early from the beginning, often before Abouna arrived to church. Thanks be to the Lord, who gives medicine for every sickness and heals with all blessings. Towards the end of elementary school, my self-image and self-confidence improved a little and the main reason was Sunday school and deaconship. I was still suffering

---
*Tonya is the robe deacons wear during liturgy
**"Abouna" is an Arabic word that means "father"; a common name for priests in the Coptic Church

from low self-esteem and lack of self-confidence, but I became less tearful and excessively sensitive. My sickness used to come to the surface in certain situations, but it was under control. Yet, I was never completely healed; I still hated my body, I never saw any worth for myself, and I didn't trust myself.

Lack of Sexual Education

Like every child, I started getting curious and I asked the famous question: how did I come into this world? I recall asking my father this question several times, and I always received the same answer: "We picked a mannequin from a clothing shop and we took the mannequin to the doctor. The doctor gave an injection to the mannequin and it became you." Then, my father would start laughing and I would answer him, "No, Daddy, for real. How did I come into this world?" and he gave me the same answer. Then, I went to ask Mom and she answered the same way; they agreed together on this genius answer! I never realized the full scientific facts till the age of 20! Believe it or not! What's the shame in explaining all the facts to our children, rather than leaving them searching for answers from bad sources? If Dad had answered my question, it would have satisfied my curiosity and I wouldn't have searched for answers all by myself. I wouldn't have fallen victim to pornography sites or obtained wrong information from bad friends. We deal with sex as an evil necessity or an inappropriate issue, rather than a holy sacrament that makes use of our sexual organs as holy organs, as they are God's tools in creation. I remember one day confronting my mother and asking why they never answered my question the right way. She told me, "Anyways, you will know everything from your friends at school and dirty jokes." What a reasoning!

I also recall that the name my parents used for my sexual organs wasn't the real name, but a nickname that has no relation to reality. When I learned about the reproductive organ in science class, it took me a while to realize the link between the real names and the nickname. I was very puzzled and my mind was full of questions.

My father used to laugh with me saying, "I will hang you from (my sexual organ's nickname)." Are not our bodies holy and temples of Holy Spirit? Why don't we respect the temple of the Holy Spirit? *"Do you not know that you are the temple of God and that the Spirit of God dwells in you?" (1 Corinthians 3:16).* We create a distorted image of the most holy organs in our children and then we wonder why they misbehave.

I recall, one day, finding at home a bottle of medicine written on it, "Vaginal Douch," and I didn't know what "vaginal" meant, so I asked Mom and she answered, "Go ask Dad." I asked Dad and he took me to a quiet place, with the two of us alone. He told me with a very low voice, "This is the (nickname for my sexual organs) for the girls," then followed by laughter. This laughter was sending a message that my question was inappropriate and we were talking about the forbidden. Back at that time, I didn't know what the sexual organs looked like and my imagination kept dreaming about how the female sexual organs looked like. I didn't get any useful information from this exchange; the net result was that these topics are inappropriate and forbidden. Nevertheless, I went asking the most trustworthy person, and I never found any useful information.

To be fair and balanced, my father's answer was neither catastrophic nor exemplary. The moral of this story is that your facial expressions and the impression you leave in a child's mind is more important than the answer itself. The conclusion of my childhood year is engraved with an impression that sex is a forbidden topic and we shouldn't talk about it. I wasn't prepared with the right information to face the flood of lies and satanic wars during adolescence.

A famous example is if I tell you, "Don't think about the color red," what will happen is that you will involuntarily start thinking about the color red and a lot of questions will arise as to why I shouldn't think of the color red. This is called reverse psychology. The dominating impression of the inappropriate and forbidden made me search for answers by myself, away from the shame of asking anyone, because all of my questions never resulted in convincing answers.

Teenage Years
Innocent Curiosity

I started sex addiction at the age of twelve. I was enslaved to masturbation without even understanding what I was doing. The first time I masturbated is still vivid in my mind; I was showering before school, got curious, and touched my holy organs. I didn't understand anything at all; I didn't know what that white fluid going out of my body was. I was shocked and stunned and I didn't understand if this was normal or if I was sick. I repeated the same steps and the same fluid came out and the same shock happened! I never told anyone about this because the taboo impression was engraved in my mind and nobody ever answered my questions. Over time, this thing became fun whenever I showered—I found pleasure and it became a habit.

Whenever I remember these days, I feel great shame and guilt. Many times, my thoughts were the same as Cain's. *"My punishment is greater than I can bear" (Genesis 4:13).* I felt hopeless! But I said to myself, I am not any better than King David or Solomon; quite the opposite, I am not worthy to touch the dirt on their feet. Despair and faintheartedness are forms of arrogance. God permitted my healing when I gave up all arrogance and ego inside me. I found great comfort in verses by Joel the prophet: *"So I will restore to you the years that the swarming locust has eaten" (Joel 2:25).*

Let's learn from what happened, as this shows the importance of education and awareness before puberty. If anyone explained to me the changes that were going to happen in my body, I wouldn't have been shocked and I would have dealt with that incident differently. Raising awareness and preparing your kid for puberty is explained in detail in many sources. Please research and use one of them with your children.

During middle school years, masturbation became a daily routine. I used to masturbate at any time and in any place. I wasn't having any desires for women or looking at any sexually explicit pictures. It was a mechanical motion producing pleasure to relieve my psychological pain.

I had a conversation with one of my relatives and he told me, "Why are you complaining about your parents? They have sent you to the best schools and they spend a lot of money on you; you don't need anything." I broke in tears and told him, "Money isn't everything! I really want them to stay with me and give me more attention." I am sure that my relative told my parents about my answer, but nothing changed. In the Bible, Solomon truly said, *"He who is greedy for gain troubles his own house, but he who hates bribes will live" (Proverbs 15:27)*.

To all parents, your money won't make your children happy; your children need your presence, love, and quality time. Let's not waste our life at work and saving money and then discover tons of problems in our children. We can choose to live poor, but happy—happy with God and happy with each other as a family. *"Better is a dry morsel with quietness, than a house full of feasting with strife" (Proverbs 17:1)*.

Your family won't flourish with money. Your family will flourish with God's word and when your children see Christ in your behavior every day. Playing with your children is the best lesson in humility; when you play with your children, you get to know them more, understand their personality, and implant in them Christian principals. *"Through wisdom a house is built, and by understanding it is established; by knowledge the rooms are filled, with all precious and pleasant riches" (Proverbs 24:3-4)*. If you want your family to flourish, fill your kid's heart with unconditional love, and the most precious gift for your children is quality time.

I ended up having a shame-based personality; I suffered daily from psychological pain, looking for any way to numb it. I was so thirsty for unconditional love and I found relief in a temporary pleasure. I was so naïve and I didn't know how serious my situation was, till I became completely enslaved to masturbation, which became a daily imprisonment.

At this point, an inner voice started telling me that "something is wrong," and I started to remember Saint Paul saying, *"All things are lawful for me, but all things are not helpful. All things are lawful for me, but I will not be brought under the power of any" (1 Corinthians 6:12).* The same voice was saying to me this habit is controlling you and you need to stop it. I was overconfident and egocentric, as I replied, "I can stop this habit whenever I want, don't worry." I never reached complete healing from my addiction till I completely crucified my addiction and I laid myself under Christ's feet, saying, "I am a piece of clay, form me as you like." I started realizing the disaster first at school, and then at church.

At school, they arranged a lecture for us about sexual education; it was very informative, but late. I recall a question came about masturbation and my reaction was, "What's masturbation?" I didn't dare to ask this question, but someone else asked this question and the lecturer replied, "Good thing that you don't know!" followed by laughs from the audience. Thus, I asked my colleague sitting next to me; he answered me with a very low voice and protruding eyes, and he explained a myth that has nothing to do with reality. No need to detail the myth, to avoid any link to evil. I never forgot that conversation till today, as it is engraved in my mind. This is what happens when we ignore educating and raising awareness; our children will search for the information from wrong resources that will pollute their minds. I returned back home and tried doing the myth that my colleague described to me, and by time, I realized that I am addicted to masturbation.

Later, a Sunday school lesson confirmed the sad reality; the lesson was very beneficial, but late. I went into a stage of denial and confusion; I couldn't believe that I am sinful and guilty to that stage. They told us in Sunday school that masturbation bans from taking communion, but I was a deacon! How can that happen?! I couldn't believe what they said in Sunday school because of the shock I experienced. To confirm this information, I asked my dad and he answered that nothing bans one from taking communion. Then I asked another family member, "What bans you from taking communion?" and he answered heresies and sexual sins. As soon as I heard his answer, I broke down in tears and he asked me why I am crying and I replied that I am addicted to masturbation. He told me that I was courageous because I confessed my sins and that he wished to have the same tears of repentance as I had. He also advised me to take communion a lot and if I masturbated, I wouldn't take communion.

At this time, I was sure that I am addicted to masturbation, and with great arrogance, I never asked help from anyone. I never truly repented because true repentance is a complete stop from sinning. Sometimes, I would succeed in stopping my addiction, but I would quickly relapse with more desire. I was *"As a dog returns to his own vomit, so a fool repeats his folly" (Proverbs 26:11).* Many times, I would convince myself that I am strong and capable of stopping this bad habit. I was so arrogant, saying, "If I want to stop it, I will." I would stop for a couple of days and then relapse again into addiction. I never asked help from anyone, nor did I even ask God for help.

I was truly egocentric, and I was missing a lot to reach true repentance. Up to that point, I was only addicted to masturbation, a simple habit making me feel good and easing psychological pain. I ignored Jesus, who said, *"Come to me, all you who labor and are heavy laden, and I will give you rest" (Matthew 11:28),* and I instead went for false relief in sexual pleasure. I ignored the living water that *"whoever drinks of the water that I shall give him will never thirst. But the water that I shall give him will become in him a fountain of water springing up into everlasting life" (John 4:24).* I was best described by this verse: *"They have forsaken Me, the fountain of living waters, And hewn themselves cisterns— broken cisterns that can hold no water" (Jeremiah 2:13).* Until this point, I never desired any women or saw sexually explicit material, and I had no idea about sexual intercourse or how babies are made.

Questions Without Answers

I usually went to my father to ask him about anything I didn't know, and honestly, Dad used to answer all of my questions patiently and in detail, except for this topic, for which the door was slam shut. When I was studying the human reproductive system in 8th grade, the logical question that nobody answered came to my mind: "How do sperms move from the man to the woman?" I was asking innocently, and the truth was that I didn't know. I asked Mom, so she told me to show her the science book and she looked at the book with puzzled deadlocked face and said, "I don't know." That was the end of discussion, and I went back to studying. Then, Dad came to my room hurried and asking, "What did you ask your mom?" As a result, I repeated the same question to him and he said, "This is a wrong question; this question is from Satan! Haven't you learned anything from your friends at school?!" I didn't answer out of astonishment and respect to Dad; I was wondering what brought Satan into my question? I am asking a scientific question. I didn't understand why he was mad. Then, Dad said, "Haven't you heard your friends at school cursing and saying xxxxxx (my dad used a word of profanity)? This is it!" I haven't heard this word before and I got more perplexed; Satan?! Profanity?! I don't understand anything! I was asking a science question. Why is Dad mad at me? I am asking this question because I wanted to get good grades. The conversation ended and I was extremely confused and puzzled, and from this moment on I never tried to ask my father again. I reached out seeking answers to my questions all alone in this world full of evil; I was an easy prey for Satan, as I didn't have any information and all safe, trustworthy resources were slam shut. I was very naïve and became enslaved to my sexual desires because of inexperience. *"The simple believes every word, But the prudent considers well his steps" (Proverbs 14:15).*

Dad decided to talk to me about sexual intercourse a week before my marriage and it was truly very humiliating! I was thinking, "You are too late! Do you want me to explain to you the intercourse!" I didn't give rude response because I didn't want to hurt him, but this conversation was heartbreaking! I quickly ended the conversation, and in my mind I was thinking, "You are 20 years late, I came to you in the right time and you turned me down."

The Internet

I was the first generation to deal with the internet. I was in middle school when the internet first came to Egypt, and I was excited to be an expert in technology. The first time I saw a pornography site was in 6th grade, and I didn't know what pornography was. I was bored, had nothing to do, and didn't know why I chose to write the word "sex" on the search engine. I didn't know what I was about to see. Truly, I didn't know what I was doing and I wasn't looking for pornography because I didn't even know pornography existed. Many times, I recall that moment and try to figure out the reason why I wrote "sex" on the search engine—and I don't have an answer! I think that subconsciously, I was looking for an answer to my questions about sexuality. This shows the danger of neglecting our children's questions; they will search for answers from inaccurate, polluted resources. At that moment, I had all these questions in my mind:

1. How do sperms move from man to woman?
2. What is that white fluid coming out of my body during masturbation?
3. Why is masturbation so pleasing?
4. Why am I getting wet dreams?

I typed "sex" on the search engine, opened the first link, and saw my first sexually explicit images! I was so shocked and disgusted that I closed the website very quickly. I sat down for a while trying to absorb the shock, and then I opened the same website again. I was still disgusted but less than the first time. I reopened the website because I was trying to understand, and I wish I never understood! Then a third, fourth and fifth time, with the feeling of disgust decaying each time, till I got used to it and became addicted to pornography. I was *"As a dog returns to his own vomit, so a fool repeats his folly" (Proverbs 26:11).* Let's learn from what happened and set some guidelines for parents

First and foremost, answer your children's questions. Build a relationship with your children so that they feel welcomed and confident in bringing all their concerns and problems to you. Never ignore your children and cause them to search on their own and fall victim to evil resources. If you are shy to answer these questions, there is no shame in using a book or asking a trustworthy specialist. If you choose a book, please read it before giving it to your child and discuss the book with him/her. Jesus answered all the questions He received. Furthermore, there is a heavenly promise: *"Ask, and it will be given to you; seek, and you will find; knock, and it will be opened to you. For everyone who asks receives, and he who seeks finds, and to him who knocks it will be opened" (Matthew 7:7-8).* If our Lord Jesus Christ promised to answer our questions, then we should follow our Lord's model and answer all our children's questions. I repeat, all of our children's questions. God created our brain to reason and question and there is no shame in using our minds to question. Many prophets asked God and He answered clearly and extensively. Here are two examples: Moses in Exodus 3:13 and the speech by Saint Peter on the day of Pentecost started with a question Acts 2:12. Many times, Jesus answered his disciples' questions and He even answered questions with a question to enrich the discussion (Mark 2:18-19 & 24-25).

Finally, his Holiness Pope Shenouda the Third dedicated a long time at the beginning of every sermon to answer questions, no matter how trivial they were. Even more, Pope Shenouda wrote a famous three-volume book called "So Many Years with People's Questions." Pope Shenouda even used to answer questions from children and correct wrong information without embarrassing those who asked. Let's follow Christ and these holy saints and fulfill our children's need to understand and avoid evil intervention.

Second, is free leisure time. Parents, keep your children busy with useful activities. An empty mind is a house for the devil. *"See then that you walk circumspectly, not as fools but as wise, redeeming the time, because the days are evil" (Ephesians 5:15-16).* The devil uses free time to capture our children as slaves for sin. Best usage of free time is in church activities. Sign up for all church activities and, of course, other activities outside church are okay as well, but I would give priority to the church. The most precious godly gift given to us is time; do your best not letting your children spend their time in useless, time-wasting activities. *"The rod and rebuke give wisdom, but a child left to himself brings shame to his mother" (Proverbs 29:15).* Help your children in choosing useful activities to build their character. Staying home is catastrophic. Give them attention and do not ignore them, or they will perish.

Third, is laptops and cell phones. Digital devices can be of great benefit and great harm too. I recommend placing the laptop or PC in a public place where everyone can see the screen. Preferably, don't buy him/her a personal computer or smartphone before the age of 16, and do your best limiting the hours of cell phone usage (for example, to 2 hours daily).

Parental Control Software

It is very crucial to setup parental protection software on your children's cell phone or computer. Be aware that we live in a world where temptation will chase your child without him/her looking for it; parental control software is a must, not a luxury. No one can build a house without a fence for protection; the Bible says, *"Whoever has no rule over his own spirit is like a city broken down, without walls." (Proverbs 25:28).* If you don't install parental protection software on your child's phone, he/she will definitely be exposed to pornography and he/she will end up being like a destroyed city without walls! Even if your child doesn't search for pornography, it's going to come to him/her. Satan is very smart in using digital devices to pollute our children's hearts and minds. If we neglect our children in this cyber world, without protection, Satan will definitely attack them with a vicious sexual war. Protect your children and don't let them stumble. It's a big sin to be aware of the dangers of digital devices and ignore them. *"But whoever causes one of these little ones who believe in Me to stumble, it would be better for him if a millstone were hung around his neck, and he were thrown into the sea" (Mark 9:42).*

Below is a list of popular parental protection software. I recommend installing one of them or seek help from an expert:

- *PHONESHERIFF*
- *QUSTODIO*
- *Net Nanny*
- *My Mobile Watchdog*
- *MOBILE SPY*

It is critical to build a trust-based relationship with your children and to address all of their concerns, uncertainties and questions. Parental control software is not the solution, but a tool of protection. The real solution lies in raising awareness before adolescence and creating a healthy environment of love at home, where your children will come to you with all their questions and problems. Preferably, you should install this software on the digital device before giving the device to your child, so they deal with it as a given. If your child already has a device without parental protection, installing this software will be very challenging. My advice is to convince your child of its importance and never force the software on him/her. If you control your children's cell phone and keep them busy without making them aware of the dangers of pornography, then you did nothing. They will go looking for answers from bad sources and they will feel oppressed for no reason. Finally, be careful to avoid obstinacy, which creates a vicious cycle; children are smart and will find a way to get around the software.

Alarming Signs and Neglect

There were many clear signs that I was addicted to pornography; I will list them in detail so that parents are aware of signs of danger

- I used to stay for long time in the bathroom.
- I used to leave my bed soaked with semen.
- My mother saw me one day looking at pornography sites and her reaction was to setup parental protection software on the PC. It was the right decision, but it was lacking awareness, discussion and care. We bought a new computer and then I relapsed into watching pornography.
- I confessed to one of my relatives that I was addicted to masturbation and I am sure he told my parents that I was looking for attention, discussion, explanation or awareness, but nothing happened! I had this question in my mind: I am addicted to masturbation; what should I do?
- I went a second time and told my mother, "Mom, I am very tired; I sin with my body a lot and I don't know what to do?" She answered, "Practice sports." End of discussion! She never followed up with me or made sure that I practiced sports.
- One day, my parents came home and I was all alone by myself and wearing very little clothing.
- I used to keep my room door shut all the time.

These are clear signs of pornography addiction; never ignore them. Talk to your children, support them, and give them attention. Once, I met a mom whose son was exposed to pornography and she talked to him a lot, to the point where he told her, "I can't stop looking at these sites, Mom!" The mother's reaction was ideal. She told him, "Okay, honey, we will move the computer to the family room and at night time I will turn off the internet on the whole house." What an exemplary reaction and solution! Our children are victims and are not evil, and if we don't talk to them and try to understand them, we will be unable to help them.

I am all Alone
"Nobody cares about me, and nobody feels my pain."

I ended up all alone in facing this addiction—no support and no compassion. I was so scared to reveal my suffering to anyone. I used to go for confession, but without true repentance because I repeated the same mistakes. I didn't like my situation; I knew that I was sinful, but I didn't have the will to change. Many times, I tried stopping my addiction alone by my willpower, but I failed because I never looked for God's power and help. I believed in my inner power and I wrongly believed that I can stop my addiction without God's grace.

Satan always seeks to isolate us so our strength fails. Satan came to Eve when she was all by herself in Paradise, and when King David sinned, he refused to go to war and was alone. There are many other stories where the sinners were all alone facing Satan, and their strength vanished. That is why we should practice confession regularly and with commitment. Your father of confession is a great source of help and support in spiritual life. He is experienced in the Devil's deceit and tricks on human beings. He who faces sin alone fails; Solomon says in the book of Ecclesiastes, *"Two are better than one, because they have a good reward for their labor. For if they fall, one will lift up his companion. But woe to him who is alone when he falls, For he has no one to help him up. ... And a threefold cord is not quickly broken"* (Ecclesiastes 4:9-12).

The Devil had completely succeeded in isolating me from sources of help and support. I wasn't committed enough in confession and I didn't have a spiritual mentor to guide me in my spiritual matters. Bishop Youanes, in his book *The Paradise of the Spirit*, recommends going for confession every 15 days for beginners in the spiritual life. This is extremely correct because no one can handle spiritual warfare by himself, and confession is a source of support and power in facing the Devil's war. If you are suffering from addiction, I strongly recommend committing to confession every 15 days in your battle against addiction. Parents also, please follow your child's confession and encourage him or her, with all possible means, to commit to confession. Without confession, your children will have a high chance of losing their purity and chastity war. The best way for parents to encourage their children for confession is to make your children see you committed to confession also.

God wanted me to go through the battle alone so that I may learn much from that repentance journey. I learned the secret to addiction healing is uncovering and exposing sin— exposing sin in confession and uncovering sin to a trusted partner or counselor. As long as your addiction is hidden, there is no chance for recovery. "*He who covers his sins will not prosper, But whoever confesses and forsakes them will have mercy (Proverbs 28:13)*. I learned to never tolerate any evil or anything resembling evil. *"Abstain from every form of evil" (1 Thessalonians 5:22)*. I learned to keep my senses pure and never contaminate my mind or thinking with evil thoughts or imaginations *"The lamp of the body is the eye. If therefore your eye is good, your whole body will be full of light. But if your eye is bad, your whole body will be full of darkness. If therefore the light that is in you is darkness, how great is that darkness!" (Matthew 6:22-23)* I learned to never care about knowledge that will cause me to stumble. Ignorance of evil is much better than understanding it. *"Brethren, do not be children in understanding; however, in malice be babes, but in understanding be mature" (1 Corinthians 14:20)*. I learned to never give up and always trust in God's mercy. Everything works for good and there is no sin that's too great for Christ's blood. *"For I know the thoughts that I think toward you, says the Lord, thoughts of peace and not of evil, to give you a future and a hope" (Jeremiah 29:11)*. I thank my Lord from the bottom of my heart for His mercies; it was a tough, but very fruitful journey. I am sure that Christ was by my side in my repentance journey. He was standing next to me and crying with me. I am confident that He defended me from evil powers many times, because Satan's goal was my destruction. Truly, God created in me a new person in His image and likeness. *"Out of the eater came something to eat, and out of the strong came something sweet" (Judges 14:14)*.

Bitter struggle

I tried stopping on my own, but every attempt ended in utter failure. Each time I sinned, I promised God I would never do it again. The next time it happened, I said the same thing. And the next time. And the next. It's an illness! I couldn't stop despite I hate it. I used to live a double life. I would go to church in the morning to pray liturgy and serve as a deacon, and then go home to fill my *"stomach with the pods that the pigs were eating" (Luke 15:16)*. I would go to Sunday school and spend holy hours in church, and then at night, I was enslaved to sin again. I used to cry saying, *"Restore me God and I will return" (Jeremiah 31:18)*. "God, I hate sin. I love you, Lord, please take away my bad habits. God, I hate what I am doing and I can't stop doing it."

"God, I don't know what I am doing! I am not doing what I want, and what I hate, I am doing. Since I am doing what I hate, I acknowledge that your word in the Bible is the truth. Then it is not me doing what I hate, but the sin residing in me. I am sure that nothing good is residing in me, in my body. I have the intention to listen to your commandments but I can't. I am not doing the truth and goodness that I want, but the evil and defilement that I don't want.

Since I am doing what I hate, then it's not me doing it; it's the sin residing in me. Each time I try to obey your commandment, I find evil right in front of me.

I love God and naturally love to listen to His commandments, but each time I find evil in me fighting God's word and enslaving me to sin"**

"O wretched man that I am! Who will deliver me from this body of death? I thank God—through Jesus Christ our Lord! So then, with the mind I myself serve the law of God, but with the flesh the law of sin." (Romans 7:24-25)

Opposite Sex

While dealing with opposite sex, I was mainly evasive and shy. I never dared to have a long conversation with a girl or create any friendship. I talked to girls only when needed, and I frequently avoided talking altogether! I had feelings towards many girls, but I always suppressed my feelings; the reason was a lack of self-confidence. My friends at school used to be proud of their romantic adventures and tell me about them, but I always thought that I am full of flaws. I preferred to not put myself in an embarrassing situation because I figured that girls don't like me. I was afraid of failure and decided to completely withdraw from the opposite sex, a decision not based on a mature choice, but made out of

---

** This passage is inspired by Romans 7:15-25

weakness and low self-esteem. I therefore compensated for that by consuming pornographic images.

I compensated by indulging myself in online chat programs. I never dared to talk to girls in reality, so I talked to them in a virtual world. I wasted many hours on chat programs, but with time, lost confidence in chatting because it was full of lies. Shame dominated me completely, to the point where I couldn't dare to look in any girl's eyes—not out of mature choice, but out of great internal weakness. I always looked to the ground when talking to girls and I never had long conversations. I was like a soldier sending a radio signal by talking quickly, looking to the ground, speaking in a low voice, and not waiting or expecting any interaction.

The Cycle of Death

I found pleasure in consuming pornography, followed by great bitterness! I used to watch pornography, then masturbate—feel the pleasure then become dominated by a great feeling of guilt. I suffered from low self-esteem. I was fat, ugly, and not athletic, and had few disabilities and chronic health problems. I did get good grades, but so what, many other kids got even better grades than me. I never forgot when Dad told me, "You are a good boy." His words were a cold cup of water to a thirsty person. I used to think, "Definitely not! He is just being courteous with me." Low self-esteem caused me a lot of emotional pain. I would always expect people to treat me badly for no reason, and I used to get mad and upset over very trivial situations.

I was stuck in a vicious circle. I would feel the pain from low self-esteem, then seek fake pleasure and relief in pornography. Finally, I would experience great bitterness and guilt as a result, which further decreased my self-esteem, and so on. The net effect is a decaying self-esteem, and I became a slave to sexual pleasure, to the point where I would search for pleasure and fail to find it. I never reached any happiness or relief from my emotional pain. On the contrary, my pain became worse and I used to get upset and cry with tears regularly.

I used to stumble a lot from sexually explicit images; I was like a raging bull. I never showed this rage in public, but I was very disturbed internally. Website commercials, many of which were sexually explicit, used to make me stumble, and when I went to the beach, I used to stumble and sin a lot.

After my healing from addiction, I found my true value in Jesus Christ, who healed me, raised me from death in sin, and saved me from the yoke of slavery. I learned after my healing to never look at any explicit image, even if it's socially acceptable to. I learned to look modestly or close my eyes. I taught myself that since I wasn't searching for pornography, then the first look is not a sin, but a second look or gaze is. I increasingly made the sign of the cross over my head, the source of thinking, and I repeated this habit whenever I was tempted by a sight or idea. I changed completely, by the grace of Jesus my Lord, King and Beloved.

Middle School

Except for the sexual education lecture I talked about earlier, the school did nothing. The school atmosphere was very destructive; my friends at school used profanity extensively and I didn't understand their insults. In the beginning, I refused to understand the meaning of the insults, but profanity became mainstream and I started to understand. In some cases, I even cursed and joined the crowd to look like a "man." I was enrolled in expensive private schools and the atmosphere was very negative. It was very common to hear dirty jokes. Our talk at school was mainly about sexual adventures and the latest trends in pornography. My friends used to exchange names of pornographic sites. I was really entangled and disturbed because of my friends at school, and I increased in sin because of school.

The school's negative atmosphere wasn't due to only explicit language, but I was also frequently exposed to sexual abuse. One day, I was using the male urinal in the bathroom and one of my school peers reached with his head and looked at my holy organs saying, "Oh! Cute." I was paranoid and I instantly pulled my underpants over my holy organs. I stayed the rest of the day with my underpants fully soaked with urine! Imagine how embarrassing that was!

In high school, during recess time, I saw two school peers wrestling. Everyone was watching and keeping score. In the beginning, I didn't understand how the score was calculated. However, I quickly realized that people were counting the number of times each player touched the opponent's holy organs! People were counting out loud, "One, two, three..." and so forth! It was a very big shock to me, and I was very scared that this could happen to me one day. What was even more disgusting was the fact that everyone was laughing—both boys and girls were watching!

Our middle school children face a vicious war in holiness and purity from all directions and they fall victims to this war. If your daily life is in a dirty, sinful atmosphere and you are not strong in Christ, you will definitely stumble and sin. Parents, if you can't guarantee a good school and healthy atmosphere for your children, at least support them and make sure they are strongly attached to Christ and the church. Also, make sure they have good friends.

Healing Journey

Sunday School

I was attending Sunday school regularly and I wasn't a troublemaker, except for a few occasions. I was very quiet, but I was known for my tough questions. Sometimes, I asked questions to embarrass the teacher rather than to learn, but I later stopped this habit. My experience in Sunday school was very positive. I grew and learned from reverent, faithful teachers. Sunday school lessons were always a source of comfort and hope in repentance. I never forget the story of Saint Moses the Black or Saint Mary the Coptic. The most comforting story I heard was the following:

> There was a hermit monk living in a cave and every two to three days, Satan came to him in the shape of a beautiful woman, made him commit adultery, then left him alone. The monk would bend on his knees and pray to God with tears. He truly repented and he used to say, "Satan is attacking me with the weapon of adultery and I will fight back with the weapon of hope and belief in God's mercy; let's see who wins —God's mercy or adultery."
>
> After two days, Satan would show up again and make him sin and the monk would bend on his knees and repent to God. The monk stayed in this situation for 17 years! Can you believe it?!
>
> After 17 years, Satan appeared to him in his real, ugly appearance and told him, "I am tired of you! You don't want to give up! Aren't you losing hope and faith in yourself? I decided to stop attacking you because if I keep on tempting you, you will get the crown of hope and I wanted you to lose all your crowns, forever."
>
> After this, Satan stopped attacking him and he lived peacefully and rested in peace.

I will never forget the lesson we took about confession. I still recall the teacher's facial expressions when he said, "Repentance changes fornicators into virgins." Truly, these words came at the right time and gave me hope to repent and believe in God each time I sinned. I recall a lesson called the simple eye and the teacher talked about pornography. He said that whenever someone opens a pornographic website, he is precisely pouring a garbage can on top of his head.

Sunday school was a very positive experience, but I believe the church was kind of slow in reacting to the sexual war on our children. Also, Sunday school was lacking activities like choir and theater. These activities build character and can be used equally by the Spirit of God to serve individuals, just as the traditional hymns and Sunday school classes.

Camping and Adventure

I was so excited to join the YMCA summer camp in middle school. The camp was in Alexandria, and I was eager to camp and experience self-dependence. In camping, I found a great relief from the shame that besieged me every day.

I was having a great internal struggle; I hated my situation as a chubby introvert, but I tried many times to change this and I failed. I tried sports and I failed! I tried joining a group of friends at school and I failed. Unfortunately, the entire school had the impression that I was complicated and therefore, nobody wanted to deal with me. Moreover, I was told this bluntly to my face and I didn't have the power to defend myself. God created us as children to play, discover, have fun, and interact with each other, not sit in front of the TV or computer or smartphone, only to gain negative experiences. I fell victim to TV programs. I used to spend most of the day watching and receiving without any reaction, and I wasn't able to communicate and deal with other people. Also, rarely did I practice any sports. The result was that I became a fainthearted, complicated personality, while being addicted to masturbation and pornography as a form of compensation for low self-esteem.

The YMCA summer camp was the only available tool to return back to a normal kid. It was a new page without any previous negative experience. In this activity, I received a warm welcome from leaders and they accepted me as I was. The leaders were young, so I related to them and found a role model in them. I loved the leaders because they played with me. I never heard any negative comment about my body or character. On the contrary, they were loving and encouraging.

I integrated easily and loved it for two reasons.

First, creativity and change always kept me alert and looking forward for each new activity.

Second, seeing everything new made me excited, and I ignored all previous negative experiences and gained self-confidence. For example, I used to hate playing soccer because I wasn't good at it and always received a ton of negative comments when I played. However, we never played soccer in the YMCA; they were all new games, never seen before.

I really loved playing in the YMCA; I rediscovered the child inside me. I compensated for all the years lost, walking alone during recess, eating my sandwiches. My self-confidence increased and I was telling myself, "I am not that bad! I know how to play well!" I will never forget one time, we were playing a game that relies on speed. I am not a fast runner, but I used my brain and thinking to take advantage of a gap in the opposite team, helping my team win. The leaders greeted me after I was done and I still recall them saying, "Excellent Job Lazarus! I am so happy for you!" As time went on, my self-confidence increased dramatically and I became very committed and enthusiastic to the YMCA, never missing an activity, camp or day trip! Truly, games and playing healed my inner hurt and increased my self-esteem.

I made true friends—friendships based on mutual respect and honest love. Campfire, spiritual talks, and meditations that we used to share and discuss, all of these are engraved in my mind. We climbed Mount Sinai in Saint Catherine. I am sure that about 60 % of my low self-esteem was healed because of camping. I was so happy that I finally have friends and I was accepted. I never forgot the words of encouragement and appreciation about my personal qualities and skills.

My friends helped me reconcile with soccer. I used to hate soccer, but because of their encouragement, I became a good goalkeeper and helped my team win. My friends encouraged me with simple, but very effective words. During free time in the camps, all the children used to play soccer, but I never participated because I was chubby and was not good at sports. I used to sit on the sidelines and watch. One of my friends told me, "Lazarus! Come play with us!" I trusted my friends to not say negative words about me, and the leaders' supervision made me comfortable because they didn't allow any bullying. I hesitated for a while, and then I joined the game and I rediscovered myself! Yes, I can play soccer! I am a good goalkeeper! I even gained a sense of humor and changed from a complicated, sad person to a funny joker.

I have no credit at all in this change, but it was God who used different means to heal my soul. Whenever I meditate on how God changed my life completely, I would say, "Your measures exceed our minds and understanding." While I was sitting alone, bonded in chains, crying about my situation, He was working quietly in the background and preparing the means to healing all of my wounds. The Holy Scripture truly says, *"What I am doing you do not understand now, but you will know after this" (John 13:7).* We usually want a quick fix to our problems and blame Christ for being too slow, but in reality, we are being carried and God is preparing a solid rescue plan that exceeds all our expectations. Frequently during tribulations, we lose our faith in God and sit hopelessly crying, while Jesus is sitting next to us saying, *"Do not be afraid; only believe, and she will be made well" (Luke 8:50).*

Believe it or not, camping created a leader in me. This guy, who was psychologically disturbed and socially rejected, became a leader! This is the power of Jesus in our lives; this is grace; this is what a true miracle is. My leaders recommended that I be a leader, and I joined a leadership training camp in 9th grade. It was a great experience and I learned a lot from serving at a young age. I learned how to deal with children, prepare a program, prepare for activities, and manage time. All of this was engraved in my mind at young age. I was leading with great zeal and honesty, and my experience leading children taught me the humility that I desperately needed.

Why would a pornography and masturbation addict need humility? I found the answer in *Paradise of the Spirit* by His Grace Bishop Youanes, in the chapter "Life of Purity." It says:

"Divine Grace departs from the proud person because of his/her pride and he/she falls into sin. God permits that in order for him/her to humiliate himself/herself and realize his/her weakness and leave his/her pride.

There is no greater sin which humiliates a person with inflated ego in his/her spiritual life as the sin of sexual immorality, so horrible that it is sometimes known as the sin of impurity. St. John El-Dargy said, "If you are not purified from the glorification, you will not overcome the pains of sexual immorality or any of the other pains." He also said, "No one overcomes his/her body except he/she who crushes his heart, and no one crushes his/her heart except he/she who dies to his/her desires." The saintly Fathers said, "Whoever brags about his/her piety falls in the sin of sexual immorality, and whoever brags about his/her knowledge falls in the sin of blasphemy."

Unfortunately, our society feeds the ego extensively. Ease and availability of information, in addition to new innovations like smartphones and other devices, nourish individuality and are undoubtedly direct reasons for the increase of sexual sins these days.

One of the best situations that humbled me happened during a summer camp. I was a team leader and the kids wanted to buy snacks from the cafeteria. I escorted my team to the cafeteria to buy whatever they wanted, but I didn't buy anything because I had no money. The children's reaction was better than mine and I learned from them. They insisted on buying me snacks. Even more, they decided to make a rule that each member of the team will invite the whole team for snacks one day! Each day in the camp, a team member went to the cafeteria and bought goodies for the whole team. I remember getting two bottles of soda, a bag of chips and cookies for free! I didn't pay a penny—the children paid for everything. It was a teachable moment about generosity and sharing. What the children came up with, I never thought of before.

Often, leadership is a lesson for the leaders more than for the children. Finally, camping helped me fight pornography and masturbation because I was isolated during summer camps from pornography. Being in a healthy atmosphere helped stop my addiction, even if for a little while.

My Father of Confession

The first time I confessed is still engraved in my mind. I remember the exact place and time I confessed, and I felt extremely happy after! I was convinced of the importance of confession, but I lacked a role model to follow or someone to encourage me to confess. My main problem was that I did not see my parents going for confession. Satan was actively fighting my confession and it wasn't by chance that I ended up going for confession twice a year.

I wasted years without going to confession, and then I got acquainted with a holy man of God and I confessed regularly with him. My father of confession was so encouraging and I really loved his sincere follow-ups about my spiritual status. He used to regularly call me on the phone, and many times, he rebuked me for skipping confession. I used to love his phone calls, which always made me happy. He never prohibited me from having communion, but on the contrary, asked me to have communion as much as possible. Talks with him were very enjoyable, and I learned many spiritual concepts from him. I confessed all my sins and he was so compassionate.

I recall the first time I told him that I was addicted to masturbation and pornography. He explained to me, with gentleness and caring love, all the dangers of this addiction. I couldn't stand these dangers and I told him to stop. I was convinced that what I was doing was wrong, but my willpower was very weak and my spirituality was very shallow. Going to confession relieved me of the burden of guilt and low self-esteem. Confession gave me a morale boost to move forward and resist evil.

I was wrong whenever I decided to postpone confession, as I wanted to wait until I was able to tell Abouna, "I am free from my addiction." Postponing confession didn't help in any way; on the contrary, I indulged more in sin. My father of confession taught me that whenever you are dirty, you must go quickly and "shower;" don't stay dirty. However, I didn't like to "shower," and things got worse because I always postponed confession.

My confession wasn't effective because I was lazy in following Abouna's advice. My father of confession advised me to pray certain prayers from the Agpeya and I didn't. He advised me to stop watching pornography and I didn't. I went to confession seeking only forgiveness, but not willing to do any effort to get healing from my disease. I was a lazy patient who did not take his medication and wondered why I was not getting better. I didn't *"bear fruits worthy of repentance" (Matthew 3:8)*.

Deaconship

I diligently attended liturgy every week and I never stopped serving as a deacon. In the beginning, I felt that I should stop serving as a deacon because I was sinful and unworthy, but my father of confession convinced me that liturgy is a source of healing from my addiction. I believed the words of my father of confession, and I had communion every week. Truly, it was a great source of healing and comfort.

I was convinced that I wasn't worthy of serving as a deacon, but I went to liturgy as a patient seeking help in a hospital. I believed that the healing for my spiritual illness was in communion, and I prayed frequently that God may accept my repentance and have mercy on me during liturgy. I repeatedly wrote a piece of paper that said, "Please God, help me stop my addiction and have mercy on me" and left it on the altar. One day, I saw the priest reading this paper and then placing it under the paten. I was so joyful, and I knew my supplication has reached heaven.

Spiritual Readings

Our church is truly rich in spiritual writers, and my generation is truly lucky to have been raised in a society with many talented, holy Coptic authors. When I was young, I hated reading, just like everyone else in my generation, and the main reason was school. We suffered a lot during school time, and besides what was forced on us to study for school, I didn't want to see any books.

What changed my view of reading was one of my relatives named Paul. He was a bookworm and had a very attractive personality. Paul's discussions were enjoyable, informative, and inspiring to my mind and spirit. Paul repeatedly encouraged me to read, and he used to say, frankly, "The secret of my success and charisma is reading." I enjoyed talking to Paul because he was very knowledgeable in everything, but what I enjoyed the most was his spiritual talks about the Bible and church history. At a certain time, Paul lived in our house for a couple of months and I saw him on a daily basis holding a book and reading for hours, and this image became imprinted in my mind. Paul overcame the negative impression I had about reading and I started to love reading.

The book that touched my heart the most was *Life of Repentance and Purity* by His Holiness Pope Shenouda III. I read this book while indulging in addiction to masturbation and pornography, and it helped me to truly repent. I would love to quote the best part that really touched me in this book.

> "There are kind hearts that cannot stand to leave God at the doorstep, but get up and open to Him without delay, dreaming of hearing His divine voice. Here are some examples of kind hearts. The gentle and kind-hearted Saint Augustine spent a long period away from God because the divine voice was not clear to him. When he realized it, he complied with it that very night with all his heart and feelings, and became a saint. Mary of Egypt remained far from God for a long time, and far from His voice. Yet when she felt the voice of God calling her at the holy icon, she was completely changed. She yielded to the Lord and spent the rest of her life in His love. In the same way, Pelagia was influenced by the mere sight of the saints, and by a single sermon she heard. She had a gentle heart that was easily

influenced. In spite of her fornication and wealth, she repented quickly. Her yielding to God was amazing.

What is amazing in these stories of repentance is how fornicators yield to the Lord quickly. In fact, this is not strange, because most of these fornicators did not have hard hearts. They had, instead, emotional hearts, which yielded to love quickly. However, these hearts went astray when they directed their feelings toward the body. The body defeated them. When they found true love from God, or from His saints, they returned quickly. Compassion and love were already there, but they lacked guidance and direction. This is contrary to those of hard hearts who did not respond quickly, and might never respond at all. Therefore, the Lord rightly said to some of the elders of the Jews who were hard-hearted: "Assuredly, I say to you that tax collectors and harlots enter the kingdom of God before you" (Matthew 21.31).

How wonderful it is that many fornicators were transformed from sinners into saints! When the burning compassion they had was directed to God, their hearts were inflamed with His love. They were capable of reaching the life of holiness quickly. Besides Augustine, Mary of Egypt, and Pelagia, we may talk about other sinners who responded to the Lord quickly, and were transformed into saints: for example, Saint Baeesa, Saint Thais, Saint Martha, Saint Mary the niece of Saint Abraham the solitary, Saint Evdokia, and many others? Male examples include Saint Jacob the Struggler, Saint Timothy the Anchorite, and Saint Oghris at the start of his life. None of them required much effort from God in their return to Him. God did not have to beseech them, nor call them with persistence."

Pope Shenouda's words gave me a lot of hope and made me find a role model in these saints who overcame fornication. Fornication fills you with great feelings of shame and disgrace. It kills your self-esteem and makes you live enslaved to faintheartedness. It makes you go in a vicious circle to search for your self-worth, and whenever you improve, Satan comes and humiliates you with your shameful past. I was truly hungry for love and I didn't fulfill this hunger in the right direction. I deviated to pornography and masturbation.

I found great hope in healing and comfort from Pope Shenouda's book. Pornography addicts and fornicators are crucially in need of hope in their spiritual war. Truly, what kept me going were the examples I saw in these saints and the many words of encouragement from many sources saying the same thing: "There is hope." Without hope, I would have perished. Treat pornography addicts with pure love and give them hope in healing. Many of them are victims of harsh circumstances.

My dear beloved pornography addict, I offer you some important advice, all of which are quoted from this precious reference. I strongly encourage you to read this book, or at least some of its chapters.

To truly repent:

First: Sit with yourself

In this session, you will confess to God your weaknesses and sins. You acknowledge your weaknesses to obtain power from Him. Confess, reveal with regret all your sins, and He will grant you absolution and forgiveness. Reveal them by praying with a contrite heart, as David did previously: "Purge me with hyssop, and I shall be clean; wash me and I shall be whiter than snow" (Psalm 50). You will come out of this session ready to confess these sins before the priest, so that he may read over you the prayer of absolution, advise you as to what is required, and allow you to partake of Holy Communion.

Second: Avoid Justifications

Avoid justifications and excuses. If you wish to live the life of repentance, then try to find no excuses or justifications for any sin into which you fall. Excuses will never befit the life of repentance and humility. Justifications mean that the person who sins does not want to take responsibility for his/her faults. He sins and presents the matter as if it were something completely natural, giving reasons for its cause as if there were no fault in the matter. How can the type of person who finds justifications for his/her sin repent of it?

Third: Do not delay repentance

In God's mercy toward sinners, He offers every sinner many chances for grace to visit him/her and work in his/her heart, to help him/her repent. As a result of God's work within him/her, he/she finds his/her heart ignited with a holy desire toward repentance and a return to God. He/she might have been influenced by a sermon, a book, a spiritual meeting, a good example, or an occurrence of death. Disease may have shaken him/her from within, or perhaps circumstances led him/her to repent. The wise person is the one who utilizes these influences and does not let the chance slip away from him. It is like what happened with the prodigal son, who, when grace visited him and influenced his heart and thoughts, said, "I will arise." And he arose, went to his father, and repented.

Finally, I present you a prayer for repentance quoted from *Restore Me Lord and I Will Return* by the departed Hegumen Youssef Assaad.

> "A feeling of grievance moved in me, but who to grieve about except myself? And to whom shall I complain about myself expect to you, my Lord? I grieve my soul, who walked in the immense and broad ways of the world and felt tired of Your narrow way. I started supporting evil and even advocating for it, till I became dead, despite actually living and being called by name among others.
>
> A connection happened between me and the world when I opened my senses to sin, and evil passions and the moment I connected with the world was the start of losing my soul astray from you Lord in evil pathways and sinful ways.
>
> I opened my mind to Satan and he threw his poisonous seeds in it, and instead of having the "mind of Christ" (1 Corinthians 2:16), my mind became a field for all kinds of evil thoughts. My mind was full of fantasies that I couldn't handle any more.
>
> I opened my eyes; I should have opened them to the adoration of your glory but instead I turned them to

vanities to see the world's filthiness and evil lusts. I forgot Solomon's words: "Indeed all was vanity and grasping for the wind" (Ecclesiastes 2:11). I removed simplicity from my eyes, so they examined everything critically, looking for mistakes.

I surrendered my will to evil! In times when I was tending towards You my Lord and towards companionship with Your saints, I always turned my will towards evil, as I found myself doing evil while my will was captive asking for good and was unable to do it.

Yes, God, a contact happened between me and world and I could have ended with only a contact if I had self-control. But contact with the world changed into an emotion. I became continuously stimulated by all the destructive traps that Satan threw at me. Even worse, I started getting his evil giveaways as an exciting opportunity with all its immorality, defilement, hypocrisy and agitation.

In this deterioration, it was impossible for my soul to survive confusion and loss of inner peace that always partners with evil feelings. I paid a heavy price for my mistakes, as I was deprived of Your friendship and Your honorable companionship to my weakness.

Oh God! Your fleeing from me fueled my anxiety so that my soul struggled. I faced a struggle that ruptured my soul and my heart whines under the pressure of my divisions. My will became many wills and my desire became many desires. I am like torn pieces struggling and can only whisper to You saying, "Unite my heart, O Lord"

My struggle ended with loss. I lost my war against enemy demons. I became broken in the hands of those who have no mercy. Falling meant surrendering to my enemies, who humiliated me when I became a slave to sin. I was severely humiliated when my soul craved sin and I searched for it with all my senses. The devil deprived me of it, torturing and humiliating me. O Lord! I was supposed to lead souls as a light in the darkness, but I became driven as a prisoner and a slave, crying from humiliation and calling to you in a moment of severe brokenness saying:

"O Lord, restore my soul."

What remained in me was the aspiration towards You as a rescuer and the Savior of the fallen, and a mighty helper for the contrite. This made me repeat Prophet Jonah's words:

"When my soul fainted within me, I remembered the Lord; And my prayer went up to You" (Jonah 2:7).

I call You now, God. Do not forget me. I call You with hope, trusting that You will not forsake me. If Jonah's voice from the belly of Sheol and the heart of the seas was heard by You and his hope was blessed in You, how much more is Your poor servant, a prisoner of my sins and self-abasing to my trespasses!? I call on You now with the thief at the eleventh hour when You saved him and opened your paradise to him. I call You today with the adulteress woman, whom You forgave and sprinkled with purity and sanctity. I call You today as a lost sheep requesting You, the true shepherd.

God, I ask You restore my soul. Who can restore my soul except You, my Shepherd? You can create out of my lost and deluded present a future full of honest love towards You. And as much as I am bonded to sin, make me grow in Your love forever. Tell my soul, Lord, whose wrecks are lying in front of You, wanting You to restore her, "**I will and you will return with greater power.**"

Service in Church

In the beginning, I refused to attend the pre-servants class because service at church was full of negatives. I was so arrogant and critical of the whole situation. What changed my mind was one of the church's priests. He talked to me in a very humble manner and asked me, "Lazarus, why didn't you attend servants prep? You are a great person and we need people like you to help us in service. If you do not help in service, who will?" He broke my pride with his great humility and he also gave me a morale boost because he told me, "you are a great person."

I became really motivated to serve after this conversation and I attended pre-servants class. I eventually finished the class and started serving. The first couple of years in service were the best years in my life! I will never forget when I first taught third grade. I was very motivated and energetic and I wanted to fix all the negatives that I faced as a student. Service was a healthy channel to satisfy the urge for love inside me. I was still addicted to pornography while teaching Sunday school, and I taught Bible stories while I was still in deep sin. Truly, *"Out of the eater came something to eat, and out of the strong came something sweet" (Judges 14:14).*

Who would believe that a person who was fainthearted, psychologically disturbed, with a negative self-image, and addicted to pornography can become an active servant! Serving in Sunday school boosted my self-confidence without my falling into pride and ego because I saw, on a daily basis, many role models who were at a higher spiritual stature than me. I never felt worthy, but service was a motivation for repentance and spiritual growth.

Preparing for the lessons helped me get attached to the Bible and grow in my faith. Also, the students' questions, which were never easy, motivated me to be thorough and detail-oriented in telling the stories. Finally, the children, who copied everything I did and sharply observed me, made me careful in speech and behavior, lest I be a stumbling stone for them. A thought came to me that I should stop serving because I was a hypocrite, sinner, and unworthy of service. However, my father of confession was always encouraging, and what motivated me even more was Bishop Youanes's book, *Paradise of the Spirit*. I read the "Life of Purity" chapter, where it says:

> Each person is born with passion or feelings. When it is not utilized properly, Satan may direct this energy to the body. Then, it deviates and goes into the circle of sexual love and is defiled by the desires of the body. Therefore, those who fulfilled their passion or feelings in a good spiritual manner are very satisfied from the sexual side.
>
> Among the proper utilization of our passion or feelings are the following:

(1) Visiting the sick: through which love takes an elevated form of tenderness and kindness. For it is unlikely that those people would be tempted by sexual desires.
(2) Visiting the poor and the widows, and caring for the orphans in the orphanages or wherever they are, and other different social services.
(3) The different spiritual services that alleviate the suffering of those who are in difficulties, sympathizing with the grieving, visiting the prisoners, etc.
(4) Teaching services, as in Sunday Schools for example, and the accompanying feelings of fatherhood, and pastoral emotions.
(5) Friendships: an introvert who has no friends, doesn't connect with anyone and doesn't find safekeeping for his secrets, will most likely become a prey to sexual attacks and sins. He might find in sexual sins a temporary relief to satisfy his empty heart. However, we advise this person who wishes to avoid such sins, to make himself/herself a reservoir of Godly love which overflows to the people surrounding him/her, and people will exchange love with love. This is instead of searching for sexual satisfaction.
(6) In the same context, people also satisfy their passion or feelings by being patriotic, or through a hobby, such as writing poetry, playing music, or many other different fields.

In addition, every person has energy, which if not properly used, may deviate to harmful sexual practices. A person who exhausts his/her body studying, doing social work, in physical sports, will not have excess body energy to fight him/her. This is contrary to the person who allows his/her body to have excess rest."

I was inspired by Bishop Youanes's words and I believe that my healing was a result of getting my energy out in service. I spent a lot of time in service and joined many activities, and I used to go to church regularly 3 times a week. I was motivated to help and I never said "no" to anyone. This was to the point where one of my friends told me, "You are so kind Lazarus! You never say 'no.'" I also spent a lot of effort in activities like plays, festivals and youth competitions. Serving boosted my morale greatly and created a leader in me, instead of an isolated fainthearted person. It also increased my faith and attachment to the Bible. Truly, the real beneficiary of service is the servant; Sunday school played a major role in my healing story.

Lazarus, Come Forth!

Healing started when I decided to have a relationship. I loved one of the girls in church and we got engaged. We enjoyed and still enjoy beautiful days together.

After we got engaged, I had to travel abroad for work, and with stress from travel and work, I relieved my stress in pornography and masturbation in a very disgusting way. I had a lot of free time that I spent in watching porn and masturbating! I was ashamed of myself. I hated myself and I felt that I was betraying and cheating my fiancée. I couldn't stand my situation, being in swamp of sin. I reached rock bottom and didn't want to stay in this situation anymore.

I decided to speak honestly to my fiancée and tell her that I was a pornography addict. I decided to ask for help for the first time in my life. I was sick and tired of my situation and I decided to stop acting and lying so that I can build my future on truth. The night I told my fiancée that I was addicted to pornography, we were in her car.

I told her, "I want to tell you something that is really bothering me."
She asked, "What?"
"I am addicted to internet pornography," I replied.
My fiancée's face changed; she looked so sad and frowned. Silence dominated the scene and I was so selfish to expect her to be okay with it and even more, to comfort me!
After a long moment of silence, I asked, "What are you going to do?"
"I will drive you home," she said.
It was the longest, quietest ride ever. I left the car and we didn't say goodbye.

I felt great anxiety when I went up home and I couldn't believe that I was about to lose the best thing that ever happened in my life. How can this happen, God? I don't want to lose her. God, I prayed for her before we got engaged and I wrote her name on the altar many times. I took my car and I drove back to her house right away. Her mom opened the door and they had visitors. There wasn't much room to talk, but I realized that my fiancée didn't tell her family about my secret. However, she changed completely in the way she treated me. I left like an outsider to her and many of her words were hard to digest. I left her home because it was getting late, and she didn't say goodbye.

Next day, I texted my fiancée asking her to meet with my father of confession as a last chance to rescue our relationship. She agreed, and on the way to Abouna, I faced tough discussions and harsh questions. I was acquainted with sin and I didn't realize how huge my sin was. My fiancée's reaction woke me up from deep sleep. I had to answer many questions such as, "Why do you do that?" "What are you watching?" "Do you want your children to do the same?" I broke down in tears while answering these questions. My fiancée never accepted any excuse for me and she was right in that. I was completely guilty and inexcusable.

In Abouna's office, I sat outside and my fiancée talked to Abouna by herself, and everyone sitting outside could hear her voice weeping and crying. People's looks were killing me. Everyone sitting in the waiting area understood that I was the reason why this girl was crying. I felt great guilt—I loved this girl so much and I didn't want to be a source of pain for her. After a very long while, maybe 40 minutes, Abouna called me into his office.

I came inside the office and saw my fiancée's face swollen. Her nose was bright red; her eyes were blood red; tears were racing down her cheeks; she was looking down holding a tissue and completely heartbroken. I sat in front of her, facing the utter ugliness of my sins. Abouna didn't say any word of blame against me. Instead, he was very focused on calming my fiancée. Whenever I recall that scene, it reminded me very much of the Sinful Woman whom the Pharisees wanted to stone to death*. I was in that woman's position— caught in sin, speechless, and totally guilty.

Abouna copied the Lord's character in tenderness, wisdom and hatred of sin. That day, I saw a truly righteous, Godly priest who had the *"mind of Christ" (1 Corinthians 2:16).* The typical earthly way would be to take the opportunity to blame and condemn the sinner with no mercy. However, Abouna didn't blame me. He acted the same as Jesus.

Abouna's concern was to calm down my fiancée. He directed all of his talk to my fiancée saying, "Please calm down, I will go get you a cup of water, please stop crying." There was not a single word of blame against me. However, he never approved my sins. He said what I did was a great sin, but never blamed me. I was extremely embarrassed. At the end, Abouna told me few words that could be summarized in this verse: *"Neither do I give judgment. Go, and sin no more" (John 8:11).*

The conclusion of the meeting was that I realized my ugly evil-doing and felt extremely guilty because of my fiancée's tears. I promised my fiancée that I will stop this foolishness and God's grace started working in me. I lost any desire for sin, but my main focus was on building a house that honors God.

After the meeting, our relationship was ice-cold, but my fiancée never broke up with me. A week later, we visited the monastery of St. Mina (Deir MarMina Mariot**) and my fiancée took me to the bookshop and insisted on buying me a huge image of Jesus. She gave it to me and said, "Put it in your room, and whenever you get tempted, look at it." I

---

*John 8:1-11
**Coptic Monastery in Northern Egypt

listened to her and I really loved and appreciated her concern for me.

My fiancée used to ask me frequently if I relapsed and I was honest and never lied to her. I relapsed a few times and I told her and she forgave me and supported me. My life partner is a very wise, godly woman. I was expecting her to end our relationship, but the opposite happened. Our attachment increased and God used her as a tool to heal me.

I truly stopped sinning after this event, and the reason is the grace given to me by my Lord, King and Savior Jesus Christ. Without His grace, I would have perished in sin. Sin disappears when exposed. I believe the secret to my healing was a flood of unconditional love that God put in my fiancée's heart. Also, the fact that she didn't break up with me after I confessed my sins to her made me wonder many times. My fiancée didn't break up with me, didn't tell anybody, and supported me in recovering from this addiction. Whenever I recall this incident, I feel that I got forgiveness and acceptance that I don't deserve.

Recovery Period

The healing was through miraculous works by my Lord and King Jesus Christ, and I have no credit for stopping my addiction. However, during recovery, I went through a vicious war that I will detail for the benefit of all.

Prostrations (Metanyas)

In a certain time, I had a lot of sexual thoughts and I fell again in masturbation, so I ran quickly to my father of confession. I never forgot his fatherly love as he asked me with great kindness, "Did you watch any pornography again?" I replied, "No, I didn't, Abouna". He answered back with encouragement, "Excellent job that you didn't watch porn! This isn't a problem at all. Could be due to exhaustion or anxiety. Let's do some prostrations. Can you do ten?" I answered, "yes." He replied, "Stick to doing ten prostrations daily and these sexual thoughts will go away." All sexual thoughts went away, and I loved doing prostrations. I gradually increased my number till I reached twenty prostrations, and I do them daily till now, as they are a great protective wall from evil thoughts.

Truly, if prostrations are performed with understanding and humility, they become very effective and very close to God's heart. They also grant huge grace and peace. Prostration is true repentance from sin and impurity. David the Prophet said, *"The sacrifices of God are a broken spirit, A broken and a contrite heart—These, O God, You will not despise." Psalm 51:17*. Saint John the Syrian says:

> "As much as the person is enlightened in prayer, as much as he realizes the need and importance of prostration and enjoys abiding in it, whenever he raises his head, he gets attracted out of excessive heartily love to prostration, because he feels a great support in prostration and he increases in joy and grace."

Tears

After a time of recovering from my addiction, I was required to travel abroad by myself for work. I was still engaged to my fiancée. Thus, it was impossible for her to join me in my travels. A great fear of sin and Satan dominated my heart. I was all alone and Satan would definitely intensify his attacks on me, and I don't want to fall back into my addictions. I used to weep with tears saying, "I don't want to travel alone by myself. I am scared to watch pornography or masturbate!"

I went to my father of confession, crying like a child and it was a long session full of tears and comfort. Truly, *"Blessed are you who weep now for you shall laugh" (Luke 6:21)*. God gives great comfort with pain; I am not giving any credit to myself. I was helpless—the only thing I could do was to shed tears. I was like the sinful woman who came to Jesus's feet, weeping with tears, and with only tears of repentance to present to Jesus. *"Stood at His feet behind Him weeping; and she began to wash His feet with her tears, and wiped them with the hair of her head; and she kissed His feet and anointed them with the fragrant oil" (Luke 7:38)*. Indeed, tears of repentance are strong struggles that reaches God's throne. I don't have any explanation of why grace protected me from falling, as I was all alone in a country full of pornography. I had nothing but my tears. Trust that your tears of repentance reach the Heavenly Throne and that God sees and listens to our weeping. He hears us, and protects us. I went out full of peace from my confession session and I travelled alone and never stumbled during four months all alone. Pope Shenouda III has a very comforting book about tears that I strongly recommend. The best chapter in it is called "Tears of Regret and Repentance," where he says:

> "The person who is conscious and regrets his/her sins is ashamed to talk. The feelings of regret and grief in his/

her heart press upon the fountains of tears in his/her eyes and so he/she weeps. His/her weeping is then the most sincere expression, better than any words. A person might say some words without any feelings, but weeping is feeling without words. They are expressive and sincere feelings."

Consistently Going to Confession

After God's gift of restoration, I was diligently going to confession, sometimes on a weekly basis, and I believed that confession gives grace and power in the spiritual war. Unfortunately, I got busy and began to not give priority to confession, and I failed to stick to a routine of continuous confession. I sincerely thank God that His grace didn't leave me, but God instead sent me a warning that I will never forget.

I travelled with my wife for summer vacation in Hurgada by the Red Sea and on our way back, we stopped by the Monastery of Saint Paul. During our visit, a monk who I did not know came, and I didn't ask about his name. He gave me a piece of korbana* and said, "Let me show you the monastery." He took us on a tour and explained to us the main monuments of the monastery, and during his explanation, he meant to dismiss other visitors so that my wife and I were the only ones listening to him. Then, he started talking about the spiritual life with Christ and the importance of prayer and confession, and then he asked me when was the last time I went for confession? I was very embarrassed to answer because I realized it was a year ago! I replied, "More than year ago!" He answered, "Would you like to confess now?" and I responded, "Yes." It was a magnificent session that I still remember till now. He asked me about prayer and I said, "No," reading the Bible and I said, "No," attending church meetings and I said, "No." I was in a terrible spiritual situation and extremely weak spiritually. Thanks be to God's mercy and protection, or else I would have fallen again to my addictions. After the session, this blessed father gave me a spiritual roadmap based on Bible reading, attending church meetings, and Agpeya prayers. This monk prayed the absolution on me and I took my car with my wife and drove back home.

Near the end of the highway, there was roadwork and for some reason, the road was covered with molten asphalt, which is dangerous because asphalt is very slippery. Thus, I should have slowed down. There were no speed limit signs or instructions to slow down, and I went with full speed on this molten asphalt. When I needed to brake, the car started moving in circles and we switched lane into opposite traffic. We almost died, but God miraculously saved us! It was a clear lesson that life is short and could end at any minute, and I asked myself whether I was ready to meet Jesus. What did I do to thank Him for healing my addiction? Many times, we despise God's kindness and patience, taking life for granted as if longevity is guaranteed, which is not the case. *"Do you despise the riches of His goodness, forbearance, and long-suffering, not knowing that the goodness of God leads you to repentance?" (Romans 2:4).* From that time onwards, I started going to confession on a monthly basis and sometimes sooner, if I could.

Reading the Bible

After this incident, I chose to be more serious with my spiritual life, especially in the areas where the monk told me to improve in Saint Paul's Monastery. I started with the easy things, which were hearing sermons and attending spiritual meetings. My family and work responsibilities didn't allow me to physically attend meetings, so I listened to sermons on my computer at work and in my car during my daily work commute. I benefited a lot from listening to sermons, especially by Abouna Boules George and Abouna Daoud Lamie.

One day I listened to Bishop Rofail and he talked about the importance of reading the Bible and I heard him saying "I won't ask you whether you read the Bible or not. I will ask you —how many times did you finish reading the Bible?" This question shocked me! At that time, I was trying to read the Bible, but I wasn't serious enough. His words motivated me to read and with God's grace I read the Bible diligently. I started reading a chapter a day, then I started reading two chapters. Then one day, I read an article on Facebook that had statistics about the Bible and learned that to finish the Bible in one year, I would have to read four chapters a day. I did it and finished reading the whole Bible for the first time. I was proud of my achievement.

Then, God allowed a certain conversation to keep me humble. I was talking to one of the church's servants about the beauty of the Bible, telling him that I regret delaying reading the Bible till later in life; now, I am diligently reading the Bible every day and I finished reading the whole Bible in a year. He answered me with a stunning piece of information, saying that one of the most admired female servants, who passed away recently, used to read the Bible 4 times a year! I realized that I am still facing a long road of growth and striving.

The Sign of the Cross

I started a new job and they decided to send me away again for 3 weeks abroad for training. I ran into the same problem as before and the same fear of committing sin, either pornography or masturbation, dominated me. This time, I

---

*korbana is bread used in holy liturgy according to the coptic orthodox rites

increased my Agepya prayer as much as I could and I reduced the time I spent alone to a minimum. I chose to go very early to work at 6 am and leave work, as the last one, at 4 pm. I would return to the hotel to do my spiritual routine of reading the Bible, praying from Agpeya, and doing prostrations. Then, I walked in the streets for the rest of the day till I was totally exhausted to return to my room, ready for sleeping.

Repeatedly, I was attacked by evil thoughts and fantasies before sleeping. I would resort to making the sign of the cross on my head and pray saying, "My Lord Jesus Christ, have mercy upon me." Also, I would make the sign of the cross over my holy sexual organs, repeating, "My Lord Jesus Christ have mercy upon me," and I would continue making the sign of the cross until all evil thoughts and fantasies went away. I was very diligent in making the sign of the cross and I wouldn't stop until all thoughts and fantasies disappeared. It wasn't an easy war, but in some cases, I would continually make the sign of the cross on my head and holy sexual organs for half an hour till all evil thoughts disappeared.

Truly, the sign of the cross terrifies demons. Saint John Saba says:

> "Before that wicked giant (Satan) approaches you, make the sign of the cross and it expels him, and this way, with the power of Christ, he would flee with disgrace. So in every part in your body that Satan bothers you, make the sign of the cross so that he would escape from you."

Training My Sense of Sight

The sense of sight is the source of stumbling in sexual sins. I used to suffer a lot from explicit images surrounding me all over the place, and it caused me to feel guilty, as I used to tell myself, "I am paying the price for watching pornography." I had a strong fight with thoughts of failure and low self-esteem, and I lost! I was convinced that I was defeated; I can't resist temptation from the sense of sight because of my past sins and I didn't know how to train my sense of sight. Frequently, I stumbled because of my sense of sight and I used to repent and repeatedly make the sign of the cross over my head until all evil thoughts disappeared, but I didn't know how to block my senses, so images would not enter my mind from the beginning.

This was until I saw a video on YouTube titled "Memories of Mr. Fayez, a Friend of Pope Shenouda." Mr. Fayez was talking about his memories with Pope Shenouda from the college years and said, "One day, we were walking together in Shobra's streets and this was around 1944, and at this time, it was fashionable to wear strapless dresses. Then, while walking, two girls came facing us wearing strapless dresses. So, Nazeer (Pope Shenouda's name before becoming monk) closed his eyes and I wanted to do the same thing, but I was afraid! When they passed us, he said the storm passed peacefully."

After watching this video, I realized that we are all under weakness. The Pope himself closes his eyes to block evil thoughts, so what about me, the weakest of all?! I didn't know how to block my senses so that I wouldn't face temptation. After my healing, I wouldn't search for pornography, but it would repeatedly come to me and I didn't know what to do because my senses weren't trained. As truly expressed by Pope Shenouda:

> "This is my eye. I have closed it from seeing everything so I could see you.
> And likewise my ears I have covered from hearing everyone so I could hear you."

After seeing this video, I started training myself to close my eyes in order to block any gateway of temptation. I used to tell myself that if I saw an explicit image against my will or without searching for it, the first sight of it wasn't a sin, or else

I should walk with closed eyes all the time. Sin comes from the second look or staring for a long time. And from this time, I trained myself to close my eyes or turn them to the other side if I saw any explicit images. The world today is full of temptations, whether in the virtual world on the internet or in real life. These temptations do not bother me anymore because I learned to stop myself from the first sight.

Pornography addicts, do not stare at explicit imagery. Close your eyes immediately or turn them to the other side. *"You have heard that it was said to those of old 'You shall not commit adultery. But I say to you that whoever looks at a woman to lust for her has already committed adultery with her in his heart" (Matthew 5: 27-28)*. Notice that the Bible didn't say whoever lusts after a woman, but whoever looks to lust, meaning to look with an intention to lust. This look isn't the source of lust, but a fulfillment of the lust. If circumstances allow, this lust would happen (Saint Augustine commentary on the Sermon on the Mount).

Advice in Raising Children

Don't ignore your children

Don't think that your children will grow up righteous by themselves, without your effort. If you neglect giving attention and knowing your children's situation and circumstances, the inevitable result is immoral behavior. Every father and mother must be prepared for their children's different stages in life, according to age, whether by reading books, listening to lectures, or attending workshops. The more we understand our children's life stages, the better we understand their behavior and are aware of the challenges they face. Don't ignore your children. Ignoring includes not spending time, not listening and not being prepared for their stage of life.

Choose the right priorities in raising your children

This includes two portions: first is not overloading your child beyond his/her means and capabilities, and second is not picking the wrong priorities for our children. We always tend to give very high priority to school because it is the future source of income, while ignoring spirituality. We care too much about sending our children to school and pressuring them to study hard, but we are very permissive concerning spirituality. Or, we care too much about material things like clothing and food and allow our children to neglect liturgy and Sunday school, and give no priority for spirituality. First priority goes to spirituality and creating a relationship with God, then comes everything else.

Be loving, compassionate and encouraging

Words of praise and encouragement have a magical effect. Our children face many challenges in school, whether difficulty learning or bullying from their friends. Let us be supportive, rather than being an additional burden on an exhausted psyche. Let us make our home a place of comfort and happiness. Let us be supportive friends to our children and not a source of discontent, quarrel and negative words. If you become a source of comfort and help to your children, they will reach out to you in every tough situation, instead of going to polluted sources and begging for love from strangers. Pope Shenouda says in his book, *How to Relate to Children*:

> "By praising, you gain the child. By praising, you show them your love and also encourage them to perform good deeds. For example, if the mother says, Dad loves good children who sit quietly and are not naughty, you will find the child saying, "Mom, I'm quiet, I'm not naughty." If the mother says, God loves the good children who love and play with their younger brothers and sisters," he will say, "Mom, I love my little sister and play with her."

90% of sexual sins can be avoided with early awareness

In our time, there is no substitute for sexual education at an early age. Don't be happy if your child didn't come and ask you about the changes in his/her body. If your child didn't bring it up, then take the initiative and discuss, explain and raise awareness. These days, our children are facing a lot of evil. Be proactive and protect your child early, before he even asks.

Always be available at home and be a friend to your children

Your child doesn't need your money, but your time and love. The most precious gift you can give to your children is time. Being busy with work and leaving our children in front of screens is catastrophic. Unfortunately, it's a fact that our children spend more time at school and watching screens than with their parents, and the result is that school and screens become more influential than the parents—a true disaster! Never allow screens to shape your child's conscience.

Answer all of the child's questions

Your child's questions may be annoying to you, but they are crucial to his/her proper development. Create an atmosphere of mutual dialogue and answer all of your child's questions. I repeat: answer ALL of your child's questions. Never leave a question stuck in his/her mind unanswered, because he will reach out for answers and he could land on a wrong answer.

Your child is a friend, not an enemy

Our daily obligations make us go home drained and exhausted. We return home looking for comfort and our children have no fault in that. Your children love you and want your attention and time and they don't know how to properly express this need, so sometimes they annoy you. Don't consider them as enemies or as a burden you want to get rid of. Instead, look at them as a gift and a blessing from God. There is nothing wrong with being patient and bearing the burden, even if you are tired.

Protect and defend your child

The best defense is a good offense. The first line of offense is raising your child's awareness about all the dangers he might face. This is where the importance of sexual education comes into play. Furthermore, defend your child from the dangers of electronics and the internet, and buy parental protection software.

Raising your children requires bent knees in prayer on a daily basis

Do your best every day in raising your children and bow down daily in prayer for your children. God will bless your effort and correct your failures. When you pray, your children will see and pray. When you pray, you deepen your relationship with God and change completely to be a good example for your children. It would be even better if you can have family prayer time and a family altar. Pope Shenouda says:

> "The family prayers have their effect on the child. When children see the adults praying, it gives them a good example to follow. Also, the existence of a place at home for prayer, with an icon, cross and a night-lamp (or electric light) encourages them to pray. It also teaches them, when they grows up, to resort to God in prayer, who answers our requests, solves our problems, and heals our sicknesses."

Be an example and continuously improve

The easiest way to teach is by example. My little child copies everything I do. If you want your child to pray, then pray. If you want your kid to go to church, then go to church, and so forth. Teaching by example will save you hours of arguments and debates and will develop trust.

> "If the parents are religious, he will pick up their piety. Here, we see marriage is a responsibility and not just a mere relationship between couples. It is an educational and spiritual mission for the children - whether from the point of education or of being a good example. Therefore, for those intending to get married, they must be spiritually and educationally qualified to be role models for future generations." -Pope Shenouda

Lazarus

Conclusion

The best conclusion to my book is going to be my thoughts and ideas on the Coptic church's liturgical readings for Lazarus Saturday. I will write my comments on my favorite parts of the readings, and for those who like to read them thoroughly, see the citations* for the full text.

First prophesy
"Judah, you are he whom your brothers shall praise;
Your hand shall be on the neck of your enemies;
Your father's sons shall bow down before you.
Judah is a lion's cub;
From being a shoot, my son, you have grown up.
He bows down, and slept as a lion and a cub;
And who shall rouse him?
The scepter shall not depart from Judah,
Nor a lawgiver from his loins,
Until Shiloh comes;
And to Him shall be the expectation of the nations.
Binding his colt to a vine,
And his donkey's colt to its branch,
He will wash his garments in wine,
And his clothes in the blood of grapes.
His eyes are gladdened from the wine,
And his teeth are whiter than milk." Genesis 49: 8-12

This is a prophecy about Jesus. I like when it says, "Your hand shall be on the neck of your enemies," as God is the secret and source of our victory. He is the one fighting for us; all what we have to do is run and hide in him. I love that God

---
*
Matins prophesy
Genesis 49:1-28; Isaiah 40:9-31; Zephaniah 3:14-20; Zechariah 9:9-15
Matins Bible
Psalms 88:2-4; Luke 18:35-43
Liturgical readings
1 Corinthians 2:1–8; 1 Peter 1:25–end 1 Peter 2:1–6; Acts 27:38–end Acts 28:1-10; Psalms 129:8, 2; John 11:1-45

is on our side and not our judge. Our enemies are His enemies and He is holding the neck of our enemies and protecting us. Jesus said, *"If anyone hears My words and does not believe, I do not judge him; for I did not come to judge the world but to save the world" (John 12:47)*. Imagine, God isn't interested in condemning you, but in saving you! Our life on earth is the time of God's mercy, then comes Judgment in the last day. Take the most benefit of your life on earth and repent quickly to gain heavenly protection. God will protect us if we confess our weakness and inability to protect ourselves.

We also see Christ's resurrection when it says, "Who shall rouse him." Resurrection is a common theme in all Lazarus Saturday readings. I will point it out whenever it comes. Resurrection is also a victory and crowning ceremony for the winners. In the book of *Revelation*, we read the verse, *"Blessed and holy is he who has part in the first resurrection" (Revelation 20:6)*. The first resurrection is repentance, which is the gift we got through Jesus, and our true victory over our enemies. Through my twelve years of pornography addiction, I used to pray each year during the Easter Mass asking God to make it the last year and resurrect me from my addiction. Easter Liturgy always has a different taste to me because it always reminds me of the repentance journey, and is a reminder to remain vigilant, lest I fall.

This passage is also a reminder that Jesus is a king and a lawgiver. Please take the opportunity and ask yourself: who's the true king in your life? Whose law do you follow and honor? Remember that what is legal according to the earthly law isn't necessary Godly. Watching pornography is legal, but it's a huge defilement! Which point of view matters most to you—God's or the world? Sometimes, it costs a lot to honor God in your life and make Christ reign in your heart. Do you ask God what's the right thing to do every day, or you rely on your own judgment?

Finally, the passage says that Jesus is the expectations of all nations. Are you waiting for the moment you see Christ? What would you feel if you see Christ today? The more you are happy seeing Christ, the more you are closer to Him. If you are scared of Christ, then it's time to repent and reconcile with Him.

<u>Second prophesy</u>
"O Zion,
You who bring good tidings,
Get up into the high mountain;
O Jerusalem,
You who bring good tidings,
Lift up your voice with strength,
Lift it up, be not afraid;
Say to the cities of Judah, "Behold your God!"
Isaiah 40:9

"You who bring good tidings" is Jesus; the Lord is the one who brought us the good news of salvation and resurrection from death in sin. Are you also a source of good news like Jesus? Or you are a source of complaints and pain to the people around you? The more you get closer to God, the more you will be in His image and have His mind. Believe Jesus and ignore Satan's lies. There is hope and you can become a saint. Simply repent and choose the Godly path and you will be a source of good tidings to the people around you.

"It is He who sits above the circle of the earth,
And its inhabitants are like grasshoppers,
Who stretches out the heavens like a curtain,
And spreads them out like a tent to dwell in."
Isaiah 40:22

Way before modern science, Isaiah knew that the earth is spherical and the actual Hebrew word means more like a dome shape or a sphere. The Bible is true and speaks for itself. Carefully study the Bible and God will enlighten your heart and mind to realize many truths never seen before. Moreover, you will get peace and God will talk to you daily through the Bible and answer all of questions

"The everlasting God, the Lord,
The Creator of the ends of the earth,
Neither faints nor is weary.
His understanding is unsearchable.
He gives power to the weak,
And to those who have no might He increases strength.
Even the youths shall faint and be weary,
And the young men shall utterly fall,
 But those who wait on the Lord
Shall renew their strength;
They shall mount up with wings like eagles,
They shall run and not be weary,
They shall walk and not faint."
Isaiah 40:28-31

God is mighty and strong and He gives strength to the weak. Notice the word "wait." We are always in a rush for a solution, according to our ideas and understanding. However, God said, *"For My thoughts are not your thoughts, nor are your ways My ways, says the Lord. For as the heavens are higher than the earth, so are My ways higher than your ways, And My thoughts than your thoughts." Isaiah 55:8-9.* Waiting for God is a humbling experience that changes the person internally.

In waiting, we learn patience. We learn that our true value is in the Lord, not our inner strength or skills. In waiting, we

learn to diligently and seriously pray. In waiting, we build our faith, because if it came easy, we wouldn't appreciate it.
Finally, in waiting, we learn to appreciate and value grace and spiritual gifts, which make us stay straight on our path, as we know how hard it is to achieve our goal. *"You have not yet resisted to bloodshed, striving against sin" Hebrews 12:4.*
Be humble and wait, and God will renew your strength in the right time.

Third prophesy
Behold, at that time
I will deal with all who afflict you;
I will save the lame,
And gather those who were driven out;
I will appoint them for praise and fame
In every land where they were put to shame.
 At that time I will bring you back,
Even at the time I gather you;
For I will give you fame and praise
Among all the peoples of the earth,
When I return your captives before your eyes,"
Says the Lord.
Zephaniah 3:19-20

Again we see the same themes of Salvation and Resurrection, and furthermore, this passage adds that God will change shame to glory. Amen! The cross was a sign of death and shame, and a curse became a blessing, honor and fame. God is able to change your pain, addiction, and sins into glory and praise. One day, you will walk the streets like the Samaritan Woman, telling people about the one who saved you and healed you with a miracle. Never lose hope or surrender to frustration. God will change your sinful status and you will help people repent and you will become a source of comfort. Satan is lying, trying to make you lose hope, but God will "give you fame and praise." As it says in the passage, you will see your captive soul restored and returned before your eyes. You will see miracles—just believe and repent.

Fourth Prophecy
"As for you also,
Because of the blood of your covenant,
I will set your prisoners free from the waterless pit.
Return to the stronghold,
You prisoners of hope.
Even today I declare
That I will restore double to you."
Zechariah 9:11-12

    This is me! I was a "prisoner of hope." I lived imprisoned in my addiction for 12 years. I always looked forward for the day God will come and break me free from this prison. And God returned me to the stronghold and restored double to me! God restored me, not because of my own goodness, but because of His goodness and His promises. God is awesome and merciful, even for those who don't deserve or didn't earn His mercy. God has a plan for us. Never lose hope and if you are still a prisoner of your addiction, believe that He will come and restore you. This is not because you deserve it, but because of His Blood of the Covenant. Even though we don't deserve to be released from captivity, God will release us and reward us double fold! We don't deserve God's grace and we cannot pay it back. The only thing we can do is stay loyal to Him in our lives, honor Him every day, and dedicate our lives to Him.

Matins Psalm

Let my prayer come before You;
Incline Your ear to my cry.
For my soul is full of troubles,
And my life draws near to the grave.
I am counted with those who go down to the pit;
I am like a man who has no strength,
Psalm 88:2-4

Pray this Psalm whenever you are depressed and in need of help. Humble yourself and be confident that God will listen.

Matins Gospel

"So they told him that Jesus of Nazareth was passing by. And he cried out, saying, "Jesus, Son of David, have mercy on me!" Then those who went before warned him that he should be quiet; but he cried out all the more, "Son of David, have mercy on me!" So Jesus stood still and commanded him to be brought to Him. And when he had come near, He asked him, saying, "What do you want Me to do for you?" He said, "Lord, that I may receive my sight." Luke 18:38-41

Be strong and never give up in your battle. Keep yelling and crying, "Jesus, Son of David, have mercy on me!" Be courageous and ask for complete healing. Stop being fainthearted, and dare to ask. Dare to fight until you receive grace. Satan will do his best to hinder your salvation; don't listen to negative comments; don't believe negative people. Trust in the lord and yell, "Jesus, Son of David, have mercy on me!" and you will receive a miracle.

Pauline Epistle
"And my speech and my preaching were not with persuasive words of human wisdom, but in demonstration of the Spirit and of power, that your faith should not be in the wisdom of men but in the power of God." 1 Corinthians 2:1-8

My story isn't a poetic beautiful story. Perhaps my book isn't linguistically acceptable or commercially profitable. But I don't care and it doesn't matter. What matters is God's message in this book. What matters is the demonstration of the spirit that I saw and lived through. What matters is the work of the Holy Spirit in my life and the effect of God's word, which never goes in vain. Don't be fooled by outside beauty, but look for inner value and God's spirit.

Catholic Epistle
"As newborn babes, desire the pure milk of the word, that you may grow thereby, if indeed you have tasted that the Lord is gracious." 1 Peter 2:2

Never try to overreach or go beyond your spiritual level. Baby steps are the best formula for success in the spiritual life. Always remember that small, continuous steps are better than large, sporadic steps. Also, don't starve yourself spiritually and assume that something is going to happen. Reading the Bible, prayer, and attending liturgy are exactly similar to food. If you don't eat, you will starve and die. Go to confession consistently and have a daily quiet time to keep yourself well-fed and spiritually healthy.

Acts of the Apostles
"But when Paul had gathered a bundle of sticks and laid them on the fire, a viper came out because of the heat, and fastened on his hand. So when the natives saw the creature hanging from his hand, they said to one another, "No doubt this man is a murderer, whom, though he has escaped the sea, yet justice does not allow to live." But he shook off the creature into the fire and suffered no harm. However, they were expecting that he would swell up or suddenly fall down dead. But after they had looked for a long time and saw no harm come to him, they changed their minds and said that he was a god. In that region there was an estate of the leading citizen of the island, whose name was Publius, who received us and entertained us courteously for three days. And it happened that the father of Publius lay sick of a fever and dysentery. Paul went in to him and prayed, and he laid his hands on him and healed him. So when this was done, the rest of those on the island who had diseases also came and were healed. They also honored us in many ways; and when we departed, they provided such things as were necessary."
Acts 28:1-10

Don't worry about people's opinion or what people think of you. In this story, we see an incident that made people judge Paul as a sinner. However, the truth was completely opposite. Do the right thing from God's point of view and disregard rumors or people's judgment. What seemed to be a death sentence in people's eyes, God used to glorify His name and convert people to Christianity. I am confident that God is using my sinful past to convert people to Him. I am sure that my sinful past will become a source of comfort and healing to others. Move towards God bluntly, and what matters is God's eyes, not people's judgment.

Liturgy Psalm
"Many a time they have afflicted me from my youth;
Yet they have not prevailed against me.
Neither let those who pass by them say,
"The blessing of the Lord be upon you;
We bless you in the name of the Lord!"
Psalms 129: 8, 2

Don't be shaken by trials and tribulations. It could be a sign a that you are on the right track. Satan won't be passive when seeing you getting closer to God, and he will work hard to make you stumble and hinder your spiritual growth. Trust that as long as you are close to God, Satan will not prevail against you, because this is God's promise and we have a living God who keeps His promises.

Liturgy Gospel
"Now a certain man was sick, Lazarus of Bethany," John 11:1

Notice it says "sick," so Lazarus didn't die all of a sudden. It was gradual, so is every addiction. It starts as a simple habit, till it controls you completely and ruins your life. Be very careful in examining yourself concerning small and minor sins, because a minor sin today could develop into an addiction one day. More importantly, it's way easier and less damaging to get rid of a minor habit than to recover from addiction. The Bible warns us to *"catch us the foxes,*
The little ones that spoil the vineyard" (Song of Songs 2:15).

"When Jesus heard that, He said, "This sickness is not unto death, but for the glory of God, that the Son of God may be glorified through it."" John 11:4

Please stop asking, "Why, God?" Self-pity is destructive. I had my share of a troubled childhood, and I was put in many unfair situations, but God is using my pain for His glory. What an honor to be a tool in the hands of God, who is using my pain and even my sin as a source of healing to others. I don't try to understand why, because my mind is simply not smart enough. I won't be able to understand God's plan for my life on my own. Definitely, as a human, sometimes I ask why, and many prophets asked why. However, I am not angry at God and asking the question with sarcasm, but rather, asking humbly to understand. I ask God daily for guidance saying, "What's the right thing to do?" Moreover, I do my best in letting him choose for me because He knows better. He knows me better than I know myself.

If your addiction was triggered by abuse or a troubled childhood, don't delve into self-pity as an excuse for your addiction. God isn't approving abuse, but on the contrary, God is condemning abuse. Sometimes, we blame God for the evil world we live in, even though He is not responsible for it because He gave us free will. Why did God allow Lazarus to die? I assure you, if you ask Lazarus, "Are you mad at God because you died?" he would answer, "No." I am not mad at God because of my troubled childhood. Of course, I wish I never sinned, but when I see that I am a source of healing and help to others today, I am not mad or upset. Trust me, God will use your pain for His glory if you allow Him.

Lastly, when Jesus said, *"This sickness is not unto death, but for the glory of God" (John 11:4),* that doesn't mean the cause of Lazarus dying is the Son of God being glorified. Lazarus died for earthly reasons. Same with me: God isn't responsible for the abuse and troubled childhood I had. However, God used this for His glory. Also, my addiction wasn't only because of my troubled childhood; I share a big portion of responsibility in being lazy. God converts pain to glory, but He isn't responsible for pain.

"So, when He heard that he was sick, He stayed two more days in the place where He was. Then after

this He said to the disciples, "Let us go to Judea again.""" John 11:6

Jesus intentionally came late to the event to cut any doubt of the miracle and any doubt that Lazarus died. Same with me: Jesus came 12 years late to cut any doubt of a miracle, to cut any doubt that it was Him who raised me from death. If it happened earlier, I would have become proud and thought of myself as a hero or with willpower. But no, I am nothing and He is all. Also, I refused His help in the beginning because I was arrogant. Jesus doesn't force Himself on us. He is gentle and humble, knocking but not forcing Himself. Thank You, Lord, for coming late!

"Now Martha said to Jesus, "Lord, if You had been here, my brother would not have died. But even now I know that whatever You ask of God, God will give You."
Jesus said to her, "Your brother will rise again."
Martha said to Him, "I know that he will rise again in the resurrection at the last day."
Jesus said to her, "I am the resurrection and the life. He who believes in Me, though he may die, he shall live. And whoever lives and believes in Me shall never die. Do you believe this?"
She said to Him, "Yes, Lord, I believe that You are the Christ, the Son of God, who is to come into the world."" John 11:21-27

Sometimes, we believe in God, but our belief is hazy and unclear, or we don't believe in the right thing. But God is happy with our belief, even if it's not the best. As a father gently and nicely corrects his son's misunderstandings, so did Jesus do so with Martha in this dialogue. I love this verse: *"A bruised reed He will not break and a smoking flax He will not quench" (Matthew 12:20)*. Don't worry—you don't have to be the best believer for God to help you. God's grace is because of His goodness, not because we deserve it. Just believe and

He will explain to you the right belief and guide your steps in the right direction. There is no prerequisite to come to God—only your belief. Even if your belief isn't right, He will make it right. I love that Martha said the right answer at the end, even though she didn't know that Jesus will raise Lazarus. Jesus gently guided Martha to make her great confession of faith. Such is the power of this verse: *"I am the resurrection and the life. He who believes in Me, though he may die, he shall live. And whoever lives and believes in Me shall never die" (John 11:27).* Always repeat this verse in distress. Do the same as Martha and you will receive a miracle. Finally, ask yourself daily the same question Jesus asked Martha, *"Do you believe this?" (John 11:26).*

"Therefore, when Jesus saw her weeping, and the Jews who came with her weeping, He groaned in the spirit and was troubled. And He said, "Where have you laid him?"
They said to Him, "Lord, come and see."
Jesus wept." John 11: 33-35

Whenever I realize that Jesus was weeping over me, I feel very precious. Jesus was crying about my sinful situation as He saw me dead in the grave of addiction. Jesus cried every time I refused to open the door for Him to come inside my heart. I really feel unworthy to talk about God's tears. Jesus honored human emotions by weeping the same way we do. Tears wash our sins and are an easy way to reach the heavenly throne with our supplications. As God says, "Turn away your eyes from before me, for they have ravished me" (Song of Songs 6:5). Don't let sin harden your heart, and weep about your sins, so that God may forgive you.

Martha, the sister of him who was dead, said to Him, "Lord, by this time there is a stench, for he has been dead four days."

Jesus said to her, "Did I not say to you that if you would believe you would see the glory of God?"

Again, Jesus gently reminded her of her previous confession and faith. God doesn't blame; He is seeking mercy, not judgment. See how supportive God is during our tribulations?

Then many of the Jews who had come to Mary, and had seen the things Jesus did, believed in Him. John 11:45

Here is the beautiful end result of this story. I am sure and confident that this book will be used for God's glory and that people will repent and return to God because of this book. Even one person is enough, because our souls are so precious in God's eyes.

In the end, I thank my Lord, who saved and redeemed me from slavery of sin. I thank my Lord for everything and for every situation that I liked and the situations that I didn't like. Truly, *"All things work together for good" Roman 8:28.* I live a very healthy life with no addictions, and I have never watched any pornography since 2007. Every day, I bow down in gratitude to my Lord, who miraculously saved me from sin. I am a new person by God's grace, and God worked this miracle with me to tell others about Him. God is good!

Bibliography

"Paradise of the Spirit", by H.G. the Late Bishop Yoannis, Bishop of Gharbia who slept in the Lord on November 4. 1987

"The Life of Repentance and Purity Paperback" by Pope Shenouda III (Author), Bishop Dr. Anba Suriel (Guirgis) (Editor), John Behr (Editor) St Vladimir s Seminary Press – February 19, 2016

توبنى يارب فأتوب ، القمص يوسف أسعد ، الطبعة الخامسة ، أبناء القمص يوسف أسعد

"The Nature and Dynamics of Internet Pornography Exposure for Youth" by Chiara Sabina, Ph.D.,1 Janis Wolak, J.D.,2 and David Finkelhor, Ph.D.2

"How to Relate to Children"by Pope Shenouda III (Author) Mr Emile Bassilious (Editor), Coptic Orthodox Publication and Translation First Edition 1995

The Holy Bible, New King James Version® (NKJV®) Copyright © 1982 by Thomas Nelson

Daily Coptic Lectionary, CopticChurch.net. All rights reserved. Designed and Maintained by St. Mark Coptic Church, Jersey City, NJ

"Tears in Spiritual Life" by Pope Shenouda III (Author) Bishop Dr. Anba Suriel (Guirgis) (Editor), Coptic Orthodox Publication and Translation First Edition 1997

http://www.coptic.net/EncyclopediaCoptica

Acknowledgements

It's time for acknowledgements as the book is finally done!

First and foremost thanks and praise goes to my wife R.R. who patiently supported me through many years. Who hugged me during emotional breakdowns and supported me through the whole writing process.

Big thanks to the holy men of God; the priests who supported and helped me through the process. My father of confession Abouna J.H. who read the first draft and encouraged me to pursue the idea and actually publish the book. Thanks to Abouna Daoud Lamie and Abouna Tadros Malaty whom I met for a memorable 15 min and gave me great encouragement and support. A very special thanks to Abouna Luke Estefanous who invested many hours patiently reading all the drafts and continuously encouraged me to finish the book and publish it.

Finally, thanks for the book editors who patiently tolerated my terrible English and made it a readable book. Mr. G.M. and Mrs. O.F. In addition, Abouna Gregory Bekhit did an awesome Job meticulously proofreading the first edition in a record time. God Bless you Abouna! It was impressive.

The love of God the Father, the grace of His Son, our Lord, God and Savior Jesus Christ, and the fellowship of the Holy Spirit be with you all. Amen

Made in the USA
Middletown, DE
13 August 2019